100

KINGDOM OF HAWAI'I

Claiming It

It's not bragging if it's true.

Milton Bradley Willis,
World Champion Extreme Big Wave Surfer

Michael Clebert Willis,
World Champion Extreme Big Wave Surfer

Everything is possible with Love.
Aloha ke Akua

100 FOOT WAVE
The Official Book

DEVIL 's GARDEN

Kingdom of Hawaiʻi
The Greatest Surfing Story ever told

"The Iliad, the Odyssey, and the Bible all rolled into one"… DEVIL'S GARDEN

Go! Go! Go!

No turning back!!!

Printed in the United States of America

Published by the Surfing Authority

<u>Front Cover Page:</u>

First ever documented photograph 100 FOOT WAVE 1985.

Surfer Ace Cool.

Photo by Warren Bolster.

<u>Back Cover Page:</u>

Milton Bradley Willis and Michael Clebert Willis.

Outside Log Cabins, warming up for DEVIL's GARDEN, Biggest Wednesday 1998, "Code Black II"

Photo by Unknown.

Author photo from the book Walking on Water by Andrew Martin.

Table of Contents

Only 3 people in the world have surfed a

100 FOOT WAVE

Or Bigger

Alec Cooke, aka Ace Cool

Michael Clebert Willis

Milton Bradley Willis

The biggest ridable waves are in the Kingdom of Hawai'i

Preface

In 100 FOOT WAVE, Kingdom of Hawaiʻi, the official book, DEVIL's GARDEN, the Holy Grail of Big Wave Surfing, the Greatest Surfing Story ever told, learn about the trials and the tribulations, the triumphs, and the drama of extreme big wave surfing. the culture, the history, and the art.

100 FOOT WAVE the official book is much more than a fascinating surfing adventure. This book takes the reader on a ride where you will learn how to survive rip currents the surfer's way, learn the rich Hawaiian vernacular, experience dramatic surfing rescues and bone-chilling big wave surfing wipeouts, find out about notable big wave surfers, renowned big wave surfing photographers, female big wave surfers, and so much more...

The ocean has always been a source of awe and wonder for humans, captivating us with its vastness and power. For some, the ocean is more than just a beautiful spectacle; it is a playground, a challenge, and a way of life. Big wave surfing is one such pursuit that has captured the hearts of many, and the world of big wave surfing is a unique and fascinating subculture that few truly understand.

World Champion Extreme Big Wave Surfers, Milton Willis and Michael Willis, take readers on a thrilling journey into this exhilarating world. The Willis brothers share their brutally honest and transparent personal experiences, insights, and expertise, shedding light on what it takes to ride the biggest waves on the planet.

Get ready for an adrenaline-fueled liquid journey like no other. Take off and go deep into the world of extreme big wave surfing from the sandy shores of Solana Beach, California to the magnificent waves of Waimea Bay in the Kingdom of Hawai'i and beyond to DEVIL's GARDEN.

What follows is a treasure chest of knowledge, inspiration, and spirituality.

Fact-Checked

DEVIL's GARDEN...

Chapter 1

The Greatest Surfing Story Ever Told

DEVIL'S GARDEN

"If I ride the wings of the morning,
if I dwell by the farthest oceans,
even there your hand will guide me,
and your strength will support me."
Psalms 139:9-10

Part I
The Formative Years
Seaside, Cardiff Reef, and Swami's

"The best surfer in the world is the surfer having the most fun…"
- Duke Paoa Kahanamoku

Born to be Wild -

Conceived in Pacific Beach California, gestated on Jim Beam, powdered milk and ice milk, identical twins Milton Bradley Willis and Michael Clebert Willis were born baby B and baby C in Las Vegas on a late blazing hot summer day in 1956. The same year Ace Cool was born in Boston. The twins were born in Las Vegas (Hawaii's 9th island), raised in California and grew up in Hawai'i.

Their father Milton Eugene Willis, who went by the name Gene, was a poet and a carpenter, specifically he was a drywall taper. A simple yet complex brilliant man he didn't earn a whole lot of money and was content with just getting by. Though residing in Pacific Beach California at the time Gene had taken on a temporary job in Las Vegas.

Their mother Sandra "Gypsy" Willis of French Canadian, Mexican, and American Indian descent was a wild child beauty queen with a head turning figure. She had jet-black thick curly hair, an hourglass figure and by all accounts uncommonly voluptuous breasts.

Not wanting to gain weight and ruin her bodacious body curves, Sandra didn't eat during her pregnancy with the twin boys but rather lived off of Jim Beam tonic, powered milk and ice milk.

On the day of birth, the doctor didn't show up and on one of the hottest days of the summer, August 23rd the twins were delivered by a midwife.

Shortly after the family moved to Ventura California, but this only lasted a year or so. With the help of Gene's father, Clebert Willis, the young Willis family was able to purchase a moderate sized home in Solana Beach California close to the ocean where the twins would be raised.

During summers, Gene and Gypsy would take the family which had now grown to include a younger brother Eugene and a younger sister Dana to the closest beach known as Pillbox. Pillbox was named after an old bunker that had been built there to watch for invading Japanese during WWII.

It was at Pillbox that the twins were first introduced to the ocean and to surfing. First, they swam and body surfed with their father, later progressing to canvas air-mats and at roughly the age of 11 years old graduated to proper stand up surfing on an old balsa wood surfboard.

Home life during this period could be considered rough. Milton and Gypsy had a Richard Burton & Elizabeth Taylor, Lucille Ball & Desi Arnaz type of relationship. They were constantly fighting. Sometimes the fighting would get so bad all the windows in the house would get bashed out all in front of the kids. Thanksgiving and Christmas were the worst.

Gypsy would eventually go on to suffer a series of mental breakdowns that lasted on and off for decades. She would cut up Gene's clothes and break out every window in the house on more than one occasion. Sometimes she would be running down the street naked yelling at neighbors. On several occasions she was taken away kicking and screaming in a straitjacket.

At the time, doctors felt it would be important for Gypsy's healing if family would come visit her in the mental ward. Never mind the impact this would have on any healthy child that visits a nut house. It does make an impact on you.

Fortunately for the twins, by 11 years old they were somewhat on their own.

A friend and classmate in 5th grade, Mark Snyder invited Michael to come surfing and the two took turns riding the 2 foot waves of Pillbox on an old 9'0" balsa wood surfboard. The very next day Milton joined the fun catching his first wave on the same beat-up old balsa board. This was the beginning of the life-long adventure of surfing.

The twins were both good athletes, involved in all kinds of sports from football, baseball, basketball, track and field but it was surfing that took precedence. It was difficult coming home to a dark house after school with all the curtains closed on a bright beautiful day so most of the time the boys would go to Pillbox surfing for fun and to seek a moment of refuge from home life. By the time the twins hit middle school they were already accomplished surfers.

Home life was basically a safe place to sleep at night. Though the brothers were both good students' school was not mandatory. It wasn't uncommon for Milton to look outside the classroom and see one kid sitting under a tree in lotus just passing time... Michael.

Milton was diligent, disciplined, and focused, Michael on the other hand was more of a free spirit, a non-conformist following his own guiding light.

Life at the beach was stress free and exciting compared to school and homelife. The Willis brother's social life consisted mainly of other latch key kids who had come to find surfing as their place of refuge. While other kids were involved in a myriad of different activities Milton and Michael spent most of their time after school and on the weekends at the beach.

Because it was within walking distance for the boys, Pillbox by default was the beach of choice, however it didn't take long for Milton and Michael to outgrow the tiny beach break waves.

The twins along with friends Tiger Gonzales, Bill Fairbrother and Frank Smith began venturing out beyond Solana Beach. Fairbrother's mother a single mom would drive the boys north to Cardiff Reef and Pipes just south of a spot called Swamis. Later in high school the boys all got their drivers licenses and with a gifted Ford Falcon station wagon from Grandpa Clebert they explored further up and down the coast surfing from Windansea and Blacks to Oceanside and San Clemente (Trestles).

For the most part, the Willis brothers could be seen surfing daily honing their skills either at Seaside Reef, Cardiff Reef or Swamis' all three were considered their home break.

Surfing had begun as an escape, a safe haven from the family storm, but now it had become a sacred practice. Surfing was pure, clean, empowering, and best of all free.

It was during this time in the late 60's early 70's that the Willis brothers got into building surfboards. Milton purchased an electric skill planer from classmate Peter Sprague, virtuoso jazz guitar player and master surfer himself. They also purchased a surfboard blank from Mitch's surf shop in La Jolla and the boys got started on their very first surfboard. At the time the leading surfboard brands were Sunset surfboards and Hansen's surfboards.

Little did Milton and Michael know as boys' shaping surfboards and surfing would become a lifetime endeavor that would eventually take them around the world.

Everything Milton did he did with 100 percent passion and commitment including shaping and glassing surfboards. It was not much longer that the Willis brothers were designing and manufacturing surfboards for themselves and friends on a regular basis.

Ever progressive, Milton built a shaping and glassing room in his parent's backyard using scrap wood he scavenged from a big condominium project being constructed nearby.

For the Willis surfboard logo, Barry Castle, a great surfer and friend came up with the idea to use the atom symbol.

After graduating middle school in Solana Beach, the Willis brothers moved on to San Dieguito High School in Encinitas. Here, along with Coach Al Southworth Milton and Michael helped to establish the very first Surfing P.E. class in the nation in 1973.

The greatest influence for the Willis brothers in both shaping surfboards and riding big waves during these formative years was without a doubt Andrew Smith from Pacific Beach, a member of the famous Windansea Surfing Club.

It was the high energy Andrew Smith who not only schooled the Willis brothers on the fundamentals of shaping and surfboard design but Andrew being a hardcore veteran of North Shore Oʻahu had inspired the Willis brothers to dream beyond the shores of California.

Andrew mentored the twins in big wave surfing when he introduced them to their first diving, swimming, and waterman big wave surfing hero Kit Horn. Kit and Andrew encouraged the boys to surf Blacks beach in La Jolla California and take off on the biggest waves as late and as steep as possible to train them for their dream... to experience and surf the famous waves of the North Shore of Oʻahu Hawaiʻi.

After graduating High School, Michael took a job shaping surfboards in Encinitas for the prestigious Sunset Surfboards owned by Ed Wright.

Ed was a master shaper and a pious man. Every morning before work, Ed led all the workers in prayer.

Michael was able to work alongside some of the best surfboard shapers of all time at Sunset Surfboards including Bill Shrosbree, Sid Madden, Mike Croteau, Pat Flecky, and Tim Bessell.

While Michael was shaping surfboards in Encinitas, Milton with only $500 in his pocket took off for Hawaiʻi to live the dream with his childhood friend Frank Smith.

Straight off the plane they took a bus to Honolulu and bought a used car for $150 and drove straight to the North Shore. They found a house under construction in Pupekea up near the old Elvis Presley estate and would go there late at night and leave early in the morning, so no one knew they were living there existing on a diet of oatmeal, chili and rice.

Young Milton quickly took to these powerful waves which was quite brave considering there were no leashes at the time, and he had never surfed waves this large before. But he came prepared. He had brought a quiver of surfboards ranging from 6'6" to 8'6".

Milton would pick puka shells in between surf sessions to subsidize the lifestyle. Puka shell necklaces were very popular at the time and there was a culture of puka shell pickers who could make a living selling necklaces for up to $100 each. A few years later both Milton and Michael were both residing in Hawai'i.

From Seaside, Cardiff Reef and Swamis to Sunset Beach, Pipeline, and Waimea Bay -

By the early 80's, the Willis brothers were firmly established on the North Shore of O'ahu and owned and operated a beach surf shop in Hale'iwa.

The best surfers in the world were surfing Willis Brothers surfboards including Andy Irons, Bruce Irons, Liam McNamara, Garrett McNamara, Jason Magers,

Betty Depolito and Johnny Boy Gomes. Mark Foo and Ace Cool also had the Willis brothers shape their big wave guns for the outer reefs. One of the 13'0" surfboards that the brothers shaped for Ace Cool remained in front of the shop as a draw to tourists and locals alike when it wasn't being used by Ace to surf extremely big waves.

Who has a 13-foot Big Wave Gun surfboard? Who does that? Ace Cool that's who! This Big Wave Gun surfboard was long, thick, wide, pointed on both ends, and had a glassed-on single-fin. On the nose of the board was a big atom symbol.

There were several renowned surfboard shapers who helped the Willis brothers keep up with the huge demand for their high-performance surfboards that included Randy Sleigh, hall of famer Sam Hawk, Chris Hawk, legendary Mike Diffenderffer, Cort Gion, Mike Croteau and Greg Griffen.

Milton and Michael had come a long way from their little humble shaping room in Solana Beach shaping for Ed Wright and Sunset Surfboards in Encinitas California. With Hawai'i as their new home base and the world's best surfers riding their boards, the Willis Brothers surfboards rose to international acclaim on the world surf stage realizing a long sought after dream. In the early 90's, Surfing magazine listed Michael Willis one of the top five shapers of the world.

As the Willis brothers were shaping surfboards for Mark Foo and Ace Cool, it was only natural that they developed strong friendships in and out of the ocean. Whenever the surf would reach twenty feet or higher at Waimea Bay you could always count on Ace Cool, Mark Foo and the Willis brothers to be out there surfing it.

In the latter part of December 1994, Mark Foo would surf big Waimea Bay for the last time. After flawlessly surfing an epic Waimea Bay swell, Foo and some friends boarded a red eye bound for Mavericks off Half Moon Bay California in hopes of chasing that same swell.

Though not as big as the waves at Waimea Bay, Mark Foo died on December 23rd at Mavericks after wiping out on an 18-to-20-foot wave.

Part II
"Code Black I"
Biggest Waves ever paddled into and surfed

"The Willis Brothers surf Waimea Bay like we always dream" - Fred Van Dyke

The year 1998 goes down as a year like no other in surfing history. The weather phenomenon, El Nino was in full effect generating the biggest most ferocious storm of the century and a once in a 100-year swell. A perfect storm was brewing.

Sunday, January 25th, 1998, a day that goes down in history as the biggest waves ever paddled into and surfed at Waimea Bay or anywhere in the world for that matter. The first official "Condition Black" or "Code Black" as it is known in Hawaii's history was issued. Code Black is the official Hawaiian Civil Defense alert that declares the ocean off limits to everyone.

Unprecedented waves were forecasted to hit the Hawaiian Islands at 4pm that evening generated by a fierce storm forming off the coast of Japan heading toward the Hawaiian Islands. The US National Weather Service was monitoring sixty-five knot winds blowing for 36 hours over a thousand-mile fetch generating massive waves heading straight for Hawai'i. Buoy data recorded a wave period of 25 seconds and wave heights over the open ocean of twenty-eight feet. The Nation Weather Service calculated that waves at the beach would be 44 feet producing wave faces in excess of 80 feet surpassing the big waves recorded from 1969.

In the morning, the Willis brothers and the best and most experienced big wave surfers were all out practicing for the upcoming Quiksilver Eddie Aikau Big Wave contest.

The contest had been postponed due to the ominous forecast and by 2:30pm that day the waves were empty of all surfers. Wanting to take advantage of an empty lineup, the Willis brothers grabbed their big wave guns and headed down to the beach. Milton owned a house nearby at a place called Three Tables, so it was less than a five-minute walk.

Along the path they passed big wave surfer Ken Bradshaw heading the other way. Ken informed the brothers the waves were forecasted to close out Waimea Bay and cautioned them not to go out.

Undaunted, Milton and Michael proceeded on only to run into North Shore surfer Ted Schmidt a few moments later. Ted upon hearing news that Waimea Bay would be closing out in an hour or so had elected not to go out and did not have his surfboard with him. Milton on the other hand was hyped up about the forecast and related to Schmidt *"**Big wave surfers surf big waves, that's what big wave surfers do!!!**"*. With newfound confidence, Ted went back to get his big wave gun to join the brothers.

When Milton and Michael got down to the beach there were no other big wave surfers in sight. In fact, the beach was empty. The Rolling Stones were appearing that night in Honolulu, perhaps everyone was at the concert. Ace Cool was.

While Milton and Michael were carefully studying the waves and waiting for the exact time to paddle out Dave Yester, a North Shore lifeguard on duty at Waimea Bay motored up on his quad to inform them of a "Code Black" situation.

Until this day, Yester had never heard of a "Code Black" nor had the Willis brothers. Yester explained beaches were now legally closed and off-limits to everyone. Yester knew and trusted both brothers and if the Willis's thought they could do it then go for it but be advised the Waimea Bay would be closing out at any time.

After waiting for the powerful shorebreak to subside and for an opening in the waves, the twins going shoulder to shoulder leaped into the ocean and began paddling out. With GOD's Hand to guide them they made it out. Ted Schmidt arrived at the beach just in time to see the first mammoth waves come charging in.

The ocean waves began to roar rising to spectacular heights and indeed some of the biggest waves were closing out Waimea Bay.

By the grace of a Higher Power and perfect timing, Schmidt was able to make it out joining the Willis brothers as did two other courageous Australian big wave surfing professionals Ross Clark-Jones and Tony Ray.

Michael Willis and Ross Clark-Jones shared the first wave together, a monster wave every bit the 60 feet by today's standards. Ross was the deep man riding closer to the breaking curl.

Though both surfers were experienced it was difficult to make the steep drop and negotiate the speed and pure solid mass of the wave. Both surfers primarily rode straight conservatively trimming to the middle of Waimea Bay before kicking out.

Michael and Ross were able to ride two or three more booming waves apiece. Ted Schmidt and Tony Ray each managed to launch into history by respectively catching one wave apiece.

It was Milton Willis who took the session when he caught a ginormous closeout wave and rode it all the way across Waimea Bay ricocheting off a huge foam ball and feathering lip. With the entire wave crashing down, Milton timed his turn flawlessly, straightened out, went prone, and rode it to the shore.

Californian Big Wave Surfing legend, Peter Mel and leading contender for the big wave competition witnessed this historic ride and later after shaking Milton's hand told him he thought that Milton would win the K2 Big Wave Challenge and the $50,000 prize money for surfing the biggest wave of the year.

It turned out Taylor Knox, an American professional surfer, eventually would win the prize money with a crystal-clear photo of him surfing Todos Santos. Surfing magazine stated the Willis brothers whose photos were grainy and slightly out of focus nonetheless were the unofficial winners.

This foreboding dark sky drizzly day goes down in history as the biggest waves ever paddled into and surfed.

Three days later on a Wednesday a second "Code Black" would be issued by Hawaii's local marine authorities.

The best was yet to come…

Part III
"Code Black II"
The Holy Grail of Big Wave Surfing
Biggest Waves Ever Surfed

Over the next couple of days, the surf began to subside, but more extreme big waves were forecasted to arrive shortly. The storm data and buoy data were so unbelievable that many thought it was a mistake, as it was predicting wave faces in excess of 85ft.

Tuesday 1/27/98 –

"It's not what you look at that matters, it's what you see"
- Henry David Thoreau

Robbie Page visionary... Robbie saw possibilities.

Robert Roley, a.k.a. Robbie Page, an Australian spiritual leader with the eye of a peregrine falcon and his friend Donovan Frankenreiter had been watching the waves build all day from Robbie's beachfront house in front of Log Cabins surfbreak. Donavon, a popular professional musician, was there playing guitar and singing with the sound of the crashing waves accompanying him.

The Willis brothers and Australian Surfing Champion Cheyne Horan had dropped by to see Robbie as well as take advantage of his beachfront view to better monitor the rising waves.

Directly in front of Robbie's house were empty well-shaped peeling waves consistently breaking 30ft and higher. Robbie related to the Willis brothers and Cheyne *"If the surf gets as big as they say it will, I*

30

reckon ya'll have a go out there", as he pointed to a huge wave peeling perfectly across the Outer Log Cabins Reef.

With everywhere else on the North Shore already closing out and knowing the surf was forecasted to continue rising higher and higher, Outer Log Cabins certainly looked to be the best option for surfing the impending unprecedented swell. At that moment, the brothers made the decision to surf Outer Log Cabins first thing in the morning at dawn.

It was Robbie Page under the Puu O Mahuka Heiau who pointed out that Outer Log Cabins would be possible to surf. Little did anyone know at the time, but beyond Outer Log Cabins, DEVIL's GARDEN, the Holy Grail of Extreme Big Wave Surfing was waiting for them.

Wednesday 1/28/98 -

"The Intensity of all Eternity is felt in the NOW." –
Milton Bradley Willis

From the Eddie Aikau to Outer Log Cabins to **DEVIL's GARDEN**

Never before or after has anyone witnessed the size and magnitude of the extremely big surf ridden on this day. A groundbreaking day for both mankind and extreme big wave surfing.

It also marks the first and last time the famous and renowned Quiksilver Eddie Aikau big wave surfing event would be cancelled due to the extreme wave heights.

Every year the Eddie Aikau big wave surfing contest invites the world's best big wave surfers to test their skills in the biggest, most challenging waves in the world located at Waimea Bay on the North Shore of Oʻahu.

In order to hold the Eddie Aikau big wave surfing contest, a minimum wave size was established thereby declaring that until the surf reaches heights of at least 20 to 25 feet, 40 to 50 feet by today's standards, the contest would have to be rescheduled. Therefore, a waiting period was established.

Some years the surf reaches the required size requirements, other years it doesn't, and this is what makes the Aikau the most prestigious event in all surfing. It's gotta be BIG! Real big or it's not happening. After all you can't have a big wave event unless the waves are in fact big.

The surf forecast *this day* wasn't calling for big surf it was calling for *massive* surf.

In the darkness before dawn, the Willis brothers were up and ready. The loud rumble of the surf was a good indication the swell had arrived. With the Sea Doo jet ski fueled and their trusty tow-boards readied, it was time. Game on. But first, they headed over to Starbucks at Foodland to grab a mandatory coffee for Milton before heading to the beach and Outer Log Cabins.

The swell was good news for the Eddie Aikau contest director, George Downing, as it meant after years of waiting for Waimea Bay to be big enough there would be maximum wave size perfect for the surfing competition.

With the contest expected to be a go, expert big wave surfers like Cheyne Horan, Ken Bradshaw and others who were amongst the Quiksilver invitees headed to Waimea Bay for the contest.

The salt was thick in the air. Wave forecasters had been right, the waves were massive. The thousands of spectators, lifeguards, Quiksilver officials and contestants at Waimea Bay couldn't comprehend what they saw. The surf was pounding Waimea Bay transforming the bay into a churning caldron of sea foam with giant close outs and waves breaking wide into the channel. It looked like pure mayhem. The thundering waves were so big that contest coordinator Randy Rarrick was having trouble finding any contestants willing to go out.

The contest area was quite the scene. Everyone including Downing, Rarrick, the lifeguards and all the invitees were uneasy, tense and confused. Everyone was wondering if the Eddie Aikau event would even go on or if it would be canceled due to the waves deemed too big to humanly surf.

To be considered for the Eddie Aikau you have to be recognized by Quiksilver as one of the world's best big wave riders. In addition, the only way to get in is to be invited. Turns out these world's best big wave surfers wanted nothing to do with these waves.

As invited contestants', Cheyne Horan and Ken Bradshaw were ball and chained to the contest. The Willis brothers had not been invited and were already heading to Outer Log Cabins.

Their plans were disrupted however with a perchance predawn meeting at the local Foodland Starbucks when they met with Hawaiian professional surfer Michael Ho, an Eddie Aikau invitee.

Michael Ho informed the Willis brothers that not one of the Aikau invitees was willing to step up. It should be noted that all the invited surfers would be paid $500 just to paddle out regardless of whether they caught a wave or not. You could offer them money and they still didn't want to do it! No amount of arm twisting or financial incentive was going to make these big waves surfers change their minds. They had already folded like a wet deck of cards. Eddie Aikau would not have taken No for an answer. No would be Go. But Eddie wasn't there.

Ho continued, if you ever want to be in the Eddie Aikau contest now is your opportunity. Go see contest coordinator Randy Rarrick as he is looking for anyone who is qualified and willing to go out to be in the contest.

Upon hearing Ho's words, the Willis brothers did not hesitate. They rushed to Waimea Bay for the opportunity to get into the Eddie Aikau contest.

Enter the Willis Brothers -

The fact the Willis brothers now had the opportunity to get into the surfing contest was a true-life Cinderella story for them.

The Willis brothers knew Waimea Bay intimately, surfed it regularly when it broke and shaped the big wave guns for many of the top guns, including Hawaiian Titus Kinimaka, Mark Foo, and Ace Cool. Both Milton and Michael were considered by most expert Waimea Bay big wave surfers to be at the top of the pecking order at Waimea Bay.

Their experience at Waimea Bay includes surfing its biggest waves, getting barreled on waves thirty feet and higher, multiple successful dramatic lifesaving rescues in extremely dangerous conditions, and had earned the respect of the best big wave surfers at Waimea Bay. Go ask Navy Seal and second-generation Waimea Bay big wave rider Ivan Trent, son of legendary big wave surfer Buzzy Trent. Yet with these credentials, they had not been invited to the Eddie Aikau contest, not even as alternates. A glaring omission on Quiksilver's part reeking of corporate politics.

Despite the Willis brothers having impeccable big wave surfing credentials, Quiksilver nonetheless tainted by greed and their own agenda, effectively took control over who could and could not go out on what would be the swell of a lifetime.

Without an official invite, sacred Waimea Bay would now be "kapu", off limits to even the most devout and qualified big wave surfing practitioners.

Back at the contest, NOT ONE of the Quiksilver invited big wave surfers in the *Go! Go! Go! No turning back* spirit of Eddie Aikau was willing to go out in this eye of the tiger moment! No chance! Their reason... the waves are too big! What happened to Eddie would go? The Willis brothers were willing, able, and ready to get it on.

Eddie Aikau is legendary for his unmatched bravery and heartfelt dedication to big wave surfing. The proper thing to do as a true big wave surfer would be to honor that legacy by going out.

Milton and Michael Willis went to see contest coordinator Randy Rarrick, got invited, and were now officially contestants just as they should have been all along.

However, the other contest officials were still deciding what to do...

Contest director, George Downing, felt it was too dangerous and pushed to cancel. Other officials and surfers agreed it couldn't be done because the waves were too big and too dangerous. Imagine that!

Twenty minutes later, *The Biggest Wave* contest on earth was officially cancelled.

Amid the ensuing chaos, Milton and Michael immediately left the area for Outer Log Cabins with NO FURTHER DELAY.

Imagine waves bigger than the contest itself, the day that the big wave contest did not go on because the invited big wave surfers felt the waves were too BIG to actually surf. It appeared only the Willis brothers were up for the challenge.

But not so fast…

Enter the unofficial Winner of the 1998 Eddie Aikau Big Wave Contest, Jason Magers, and Runner-up, Greg Russ -

Unofficial Winner Jason Magers -

It turns out somebody did go! Managing to avoid the lifeguards and police barricades, North Shore local Jason Magers could not be stopped.

Magers was another big wave surfing contender not invited to the contest. So, Jason seized the moment by paddling out all alone into incomprehensible conditions.

Jason was a man possessed.

Before getting halfway out an enormous wave broke directly in front of Magers and he had to bail for his life. Later, Magers related how he curled up into the fetal position and he watched his life going in reverse until he became a baby, at which point he resurfaced.

After being washed ashore and coming in Magers subsequently was arrested, not for having gone out but rather for outstanding warrants.

The only thing that stopped him from surfing the waves this historic day were the waves themselves. As it should be.

By virtue of Magers display of supreme courage and daring to go when the "pros" wouldn't, truly honors Eddie Aikau's legacy more than the contest. It would be only fitting to give the prize money and first place to Jason Magers, the unofficial winner of the 98' Quiksilver Eddie Aikau Big Wave Contest.

Runner-up, Greg Russ -

The hands down unofficial runner-up was the big wave surfer and legitimate Hellman, Greg Russ.

The fact that the big wave contest got canceled was good news for the uninvited, albeit exceptionally well qualified, Greg Russ. This meant he could have a shot at riding these waves.

Greg Russ saw opportunity before him and wanted to be the king of the liquid Nephilim. Unfortunately for Russ, when the "Code Black" was issued the police stopped him from going out much to his dismay and rigorous objections.

By virtue of his earnest attempt to surf Waimea Bay on this day, contest or not, Greg Russ, despite being restrained by law enforcement became the unofficial runner up in the Eddie Aikau big wave surfing contest.

True big wave riders don't wait for the fanfare, the cameras, or a payday at the end of the day. They don't wait for fame and fortune. It's a higher calling that must be answered. When the waves are pumping a true big wave surfer will drop everything to go surfing because he knows big waves are unique, priceless, and rare. You can't stop him or her.

After leaving the contest area the Willis brothers quickly headed over to Michael's house at Sunset Beach where moments later, they would do a risky beach launch with their jet ski and tow board.

Destination Outer Log Cabins -

Liquid walls of death were breaking out as far as the eye could see and what seemed to be another mile past that. The salt in the air was so thick you couldn't see the outside breaking waves from the shore. It was a complete whiteout. Nothing but white frothing foam from the shore to the horizon. It was impossible to truly determine just how far out the waves were breaking.

The Willis brothers launched directly off the beach at Sunset Point, a seemingly impossible feat. Michael was piloting an old secondhand little green and white Sea Doo jet ski. Michael was focused and determined to make it through and around an endless ocean of nonstop tidal waves.

If they made it out, Milton would be first up to surf. Milton with his surfboard secured under his arm was set to go like a gladiator into the arena.

Defying all human understanding, against all odds and probability, guided purely by the Hand of GOD himself, the Willis brothers miraculously did make it out to Outer Log Cabins.

Not far behind –

Cheyne Horan, Sam Hawk, Ken Bradshaw and Dan Moore were following in the Willis brothers' footsteps except a beach launch was out of the question for them … too dangerous.

They had decided it would be safer and saner to launch from Haleʻiwa harbor which they did as did everyone who went out later this day with the exception of the brothers who launched directly off Sunset Beach twice.

While launching a jet ski off the beach in these unprecedented conditions could be considered insanity, launching from the safety of the harbor was no cake walk either. Ace Cool and Ron Barren launched off the harbor, but never made it out. They got cleaned-up hard by a series of mountainous waves as they rounded the corner off of Puena Point.

It should be noted that after the Willis brothers were *already* out surfing, "Code Black II" was officially issued legally closing all North Shore beaches. Waves so big that they made Waimea Bay look like a shorebreak which it literally was on this day.

When the Willis brothers finally reached Outer Log Cabins it was like a scene from Jurassic Park except instead of extremely big threating dinosaurs it was extremely big ominous waves.

As if out of a chapter from Homer's epic poem "Odyssey", the Willis brothers found themselves amongst a phalanx of liquid Extreme Big Waves, way bigger than anything they had ever experienced or imagined before. Waves standing so high they actually scraped the sky blocking out the horizon.

On high alert and intently scouting the waves, Michael saw a third wave coming in a series of waves that was by far the biggest baddest wave of the entire set. A blue bird so big it seemed as if it was moving in slow motion but in reality, moving like a speeding freight train.

As they had practiced many times before, Michael lifted his hand showing three fingers singling to Milton get ready you're going on the third wave and for the ride of your life.

The Willis brothers rode up over and down the backside of the first wave. It felt every bit 100 FEET. Today, oceanographers estimate these waves to be 85ft to 90ft. The second wave was even bigger, but it turned out Michael was on-point the third wave was nothing short of colossal monumental size.

As the third wave approached them, Michael gunned the Sea Doo whipping Milton into the top of the wave. Most surfers would have dropped in and headed for the shoulder. Milton decided to drop in and fade back into the belly of the beast.

Milton looked like he was traveling 40 to 45mph an hour with his hair flying in the wind. The wave was powerful and fierce, but Milton remained calm and loose, surfing with control in perfect rhythm and harmony, matching power with heart.

As the wave grew steeper and steeper and the thick crest began to pitch and fall, Milton began his turn off the bottom of the wave. Milton looked like a little dot with a Mount Everest avalanche about to consume him.

Michael meanwhile was further along on the shoulder of the beast watching the entire event unfold. It should be noted that other tow-surf drivers were riding *behind* the wave as to not to ruin any potential photograph. Michael was more concerned about his brother's safety than any photographs was positioned where he could keep an eye on his twin brother.

Yet no matter how fast Milton was going the wave was faster. Milton, upon seeing the enormity of the wave's crest coming down on him redirected his surfboard preparing to take the entire ocean on the head.

Milton completely disappeared. Swallowed, vanished, and gone from sight buried alive by a huge wall of white water with the weight of entire ocean behind it. Milton was a seasoned salt who had experienced intense wipeouts before but nothing of this magnitude or scale.

Horrified, there was nothing Michael could do to help his brother.

For Michael time stood still.

Watching vigilantly to see what Milton's fate would be, Michael became hysterically overjoyed when he saw Milton come flying out of the darkness of the wave and into the light of day. With all the courage and determination of the bravest warrior Milton had held on steadfast, successfully making the wave against all the odds. It may have been the sun glistening off the water droplets on Milton's tanned body or something else but either way Milton was glowing.

In a state of utter delirium, Michael raised his hands upward flipping off the Heavens, shouting F'ing A! F'ing A! What Michael was saying from his heart was THANK YOU GOD THANK YOU GOD THANK YOU GOD THANK YOU GOD!!! You had to be there. *A maniac moment for sure.*

What the best big wave surfers, lifeguards, and watermen in the world had thought impossible was proven possible at that very moment by Milton Willis's mind altering incredible and historic ride. A successful ride that shattered the ceiling of big wave surfing, human understanding, and marked the beginning of extreme big wave surfing.

In this moment. neither Milton or Michael realized nor completely understood what had just occurred! It was all a blur that seemed to happen in slow motion. There was no time to fully take it all in as more XXL waves were quickly drawing near from out the back.

Michael jack rabbited over picking up his brother whose energy level was off the charts literally electric and supercharged. And why not Milton had just experienced going where no man on earth had ever been.

As the Willis brothers headed back out to sea to catch another wave, they could see riders in the distance rapidly approaching at full speed. It was Ken Bradshaw and his driver, Dan Moore, followed by Cheyne Horan and Sam Hawk.

The brothers were in perfect position for the next wave which was a beauty of a beast, as thick as it was tall. Mike raised his hand signaling to Milt get ready this is for you and proceeded to whip Milton into the wave, but something caught his eyes and ears.

It was the loud, obnoxious, roar of Bradshaw and Moore's huge boat of a jet ski, and they were heading at full speed towards the Willis brothers. This was now a game of chicken with the two teams competing for the same wave.

Moore driving Bradshaw had a crazy maniacal Mad Max look in his eyes the kind of look that says I don't care I'm taking this, and you can't stop me especially on your dinky little jet ski.

Bradshaw was worse. He was staring straight ahead as if no one was there like a rat cartoon character in real life. It could have been a scene from a movie, think Thunderdome. Moore was not backing down a collision was imminently unavoidable.

In this game of chicken, the Willis brothers acquiesced. They choose to yield to Bradshaw or risk being plowed into by a jet ski twice the size of theirs going 50 mph. Instead of right of way, this was right of weight.

The wave they gave way to Bradshaw turned out to be the hallmark photo that defined this historic swell often referred to as "Biggest Wednesday". The wave was initially estimated at 40 feet by Hawaii's daily newspapers but is now considered 85 feet by today's standards.

Hank Foto is credited with taking the iconic photo that day which at the time was considered the largest wave surfed ever photographed. Hank who was filming from his jet ski with Larry Haynes is quoted as saying.

"I saw 100 FOOT WAVES that day, so Big they looked fake!"

Not to be deterred by Bradshaw, Michael towed Milton into the very next wave. Unfortunately, one of the three helicopters out there that day filming came too close to Milton and with the force of the winds coming off the helicopter blades combined with the offshore trade winds blowing up the face of the wave and Milton racing down the face of an 85-footer, Milton was blasted right off his surfboard and the wave ended up breaking his surfboard into pieces.

Michael barely had enough time to rescue his twin brother as an extremely big avalanche of white water was rapidly closing in and threatening to annihilate them. With keen precision, timing and speed Michael raced over and was able to successfully retrieve and get Milton aboard the jet ski.

At this point, there was only one way to go and that was straight to shore as fast as they could. The trouble was that there was no shore anymore, only a wall of exposed jagged lava. As typical with big waves all the sand had been washed out and the regular sandy beach shoreline was gone. The Willis brothers were in a dire situation.

Positioned between two extremely big waves, one in front of them one behind them and heading directly towards a rock lava wall, the situation was not looking good.

However, there was one chance.

If Michael could time things just right the wave ahead would cover and submerge the lava wall enabling them to reach what little beach was left. The dilemma was that the wave behind was bigger, moving faster and gaining on them. No one would ever want to be in this situation. There was only one choice they could make and that was *Go Go Go!*

At full throttle, Michael keeping his composure and remaining focused, led by Divine guidance, trailed the first wave up onto the beach miraculously flying over the wall of rock lava, hitting a sand berm, launching 8 feet high and 30 feet through the air, over a wooden fence, and crashing into a house. Surviving the insane ordeal was nothing short of a miracle.

While all this was happening at the beach, a throng of onlookers who were watching the melodrama unfold all began screaming in sheer pandemonium.

As the wave began washing back out to sea it was taking the jet ski with it. Fortunately, a brave Brazilian-Hawaiian surfer named Fabio Fejonez Rossi, Pat Gautreaux and others jumped in to help the Willis brothers and prevent the jet ski from getting sucked back out to sea. Twenty years later, Fabio Fejonez Rossi is quoted as saying, *"You guys wear the Crown!"*

The Willis brothers weren't done yet. They rushed back to Michael's place to get another tow board and upon arrival they were surprised to find Cheyne Horan and Sam Hawk already back in.

The brothers tried to get Horan and Hawk to go back out a second time with them, but the pair made it clear there was no way they were going out a second time, not in those conditions. Hawk and Horan two of the best and most experienced big wave surfers tapped out.

Milton and Michael were driven by a Higher Power, nothing was going to stop them from going back out. After hydrating, consuming a power bar, and refueling their little Sea Doo the twins were ready for round two.

The waves were showing no signs of letting up. By now the entire North Shore community was wall to wall with tourists, locals and most of the world's best big wave surfers including Garrett McNamara, future biggest wave surfed Guinness book of world record holder, were all watching intently from the shore.

Stretched out across most of the North Shore was yellow police tape reading "CAUTION DO NOT ENTER", the kind that is often used to cordon off crime scenes.

Traffic had come to a standstill in both directions gridlocked along the Kamehameha highway backed up for hours with islanders hoping to see the unprecedented waves and the surfers who dared to ride them.

With the help of friends including Pat "Big Bird" Gautreaux, the Willis brothers launched off the beach at Sunset Point for a second time and fearlessly headed back out into the raging monstrous ocean.

After carefully weaving, dodging, maneuvering in and out, up and over waves as big as tall mountains the Willis brothers again with Michael driving the Sea Doo and purely by Michaels skillful navigation and the Grace of GOD succeeded in getting back out beyond the lineup.

Once out, the brothers made their way back to Outer Log Cabins for the second time. Ken and Dan had gone in but now there was three other tow surfing teams out including Australian professional big wave surfers Ross Clark-Jones and Tony Ray. The atmosphere was supercharged, competitive and completely Raiders of the Lost Arc surreal.

In the frenzy, Clark-Jones and Ray ended up getting wiped-out by a big wave. The surfing media erroneously reported that it was the Willis brothers that got mowed. In truth, it was Ross and Tony that got mowed.

Michael proceeded to tow Milton into several BOMBS all of which Milton surfed perfectly with power, style, aplomb, and with no fear, only love and more love. Prepared not scared.

Tim Bonython captured Milton's waves on video and used them in his big wave surfing documentary "Biggest Wednesday".

Standouts from this historic afternoon session at Outer Log Cabins included in the video were Shawn Briley, Noah Johnson, and Troy Allotis. Bonython described the waves as *"Walls of Death"*.

By now, it was late in the afternoon and the sun was getting low. Knowing when enough is enough and that getting back to shore would be almost as dangerous as getting out, Milton and Michael called it a day and began heading back to Sunset Point.

Destination DEVIL's GARDEN –

The once in a 100-year swell!!! .

Taking precautions not to get caught inside by rogue waves, the brothers powered further out to sea in their little Sea Doo jet ski another half mile or so before heading back home to Sunset Beach.

The closer the Willis brothers got to Sunset Beach (Paumalu) the bigger the waves were getting and the further out they had to go.

Upon arrival to outside Sunset Beach, Michael paused their little Sea Doo allowing the brothers to take in what they were actually witnessing and experiencing.

In front of them were towering, greater than a 10-story building, wide open tidal wave size waves, barreling Top-to-Bottom that looked more animated than real.

Taunting, Teasing, Foreboding, Seductive, Scary, wide open 100 FOOT Plus Deep Dark Blue Sky-High Astronomical Size Booming Barrels!!!

The Willis brothers hadn't planned on surfing Outer Sunset Beach (Paumalu) that day and no one else did either. The waves here were double the danger, double the risk, double the size of Outer Log Cabins.

"You only get one shot. This opportunity only comes once in a lifetime" - Eminem

No stranger to danger, the ever wild and free-spirited Michael was ready to go. A powerful unseen force was calling him. The temptation he was feeling to surf just one of these waves and make it out alive began to overwhelm and consume him.

Michael had to know what such a ride would feel like. It wasn't athleticism, I'm better than you, camera on action on, a competition thing nor this could kill me 1000 times ultimate thrill thing.

What would it be like to ride on the sparkle wall between life and death, facing truth straight on surrendering to fate while held in God's protective hands like an innocent snow-white dove.

Just like in the Bible, to partake in this liquid tree of knowledge, Michael had to have a bite of that apple. It cannot be overestimated that no one on earth had ever done this before nor was ever offered this opportunity to take the first bite of a 100 foot plus wave. Michael's very life was at stake like a sacrificial lamb.

Michael trusted that his beloved brother Milton could tow him in, but he also knew should anything go wrong in no way would Milton be able to retrieve him. Milton believed and trusted in his brother Michael like no other and with no apprehension the brothers' switched places. Now it was Milton's turn to drive the jet ski and Michael's turn to roll the dice.

The Devil made him do it -

Michael had to have a bite of the apple. The Devil made him do it, as a test of his core faith in He who sent him. Ask yourself, who sent you?

With the precision of sending a rocket to the moon, Milton sent Michael soaring into either Heaven or Hell, no way to go back his fate firmly in the hands of the Ocean Gods.

If the waves at Outer Log Cabins looked deceptively slow motion, in comparison the waves at Outer Sunset Beach (Paumalu) appeared ridiculously slow motion as in frame-by-frame slow motion.

Michael looked like a skier coming down a mountain going ninety miles per hour, but this mountain was moving fast casting a dark shadow on everything in its path.

Michael made the steep drop screaming down the face of the wave while cutting a sharp right angle, sea spray flying off the chattering surfboard skittering as fast as it could go.

At this point it was less about surfing the wave and more about going straight and staying on for dear life. The wave kept peeling.

Michael's historic ride lasted for over half a mile before he ended it by going up and over the top of the wave kicking out the back. At this moment time stood still.

Michael Clebert Willis became the first surfer in history to officially ride a wave bigger than 100 feet.

Seconds later, Milton ever faithful and loyal companion from birth, zoomed in to pick Michael up.

Superman Milton had already surfed extreme Outer Log Cabins twice this day, but no way was he ready to go in after watching his brother's monumental phenomenal otherworldly ride. He was more than eager to go.

Being the ever loving and dedicated brother that Michael is, he was determined to get Milton an even bigger wave than the one he had just survived.

In this moment, extreme big wave surfing became a spiritual experience for both Milton and Michael who were feeling overwhelmingly blessed.

There was an aura of a Higher Power permeating the Pacific Ocean Mist in the air mightier than all the tidal waves in the world combined.

Michael raised his hand giving Milton the sign "This is it!" One wrong move and Milton would be gone for good. Milton was ready for what would be one Hell of a ride!

With no lifeguards present, no helicopters buzzing overhead and absolutely no fanfare, Michael flung Milton into what would be the BIGGEST WAVE ever surfed on earth with God, His Angels, and the chosen few as witness.

This wave was not an easy roller. It was powerful top-to-bottom barrel with a 10ft thick lip that pitched out 75ft and then took ten seconds to reach the bottom. Literally, a tidal wave breaking in the middle of the ocean.

Neither Milton nor Michael ever put a measurement to the prodigious waves they surfed this milestone day... however, others did. Expert big wave surfers estimated the waves that the Willis brothers rode at DEVIL's GARGEN at well over 100 feet.

Robbie Page, Pipeline Master Winner, movie star and Australian ambassador to the surfing world is quoted as saying, *"F'n yea!, I saw the Willis brothers surf 100 FOOT waves!"*

Ride the Truly Wild Surf -

The Willis brothers had escaped death and in doing so had surfed the BIGGEST WAVES the world has ever seen to present date. That's right. And now it was time to go back home.

Milton and Michael, two humble brothers originally from Solana Beach had been tested at outside Sunset Beach by the Devil himself.

Motivated by faith, love, and hope, the Willis brothers were pure in their intentions, proving to one and all with love in your heart that everything is possible beyond imagination.

All Glory to the Highest Power.

The brothers headed for shore following a huge wave right up to the beach. As the wave reached the shore, Michael revved the engine getting a burst of speed and propelled the Sea Doo jet ski onto the sand sliding up onto beach beyond the waves powerful reach.

On the beach watching the Willis brothers beach landing unfold was big wave surfer Kirby Kotlar. Kirby was getting ready to smoke a joint with a friend and to enjoy the Hawaiian sunset was shocked to see the Milton and Michael coming in from these massive waves. Kotlar could not believe his eyes. Agog, Kotlar incredulously asked the Willis's point blank "*Were you two really riding those waves out there?!!!*"

The answer was Yes. The Willis brothers, Milton and Michael, went to the remote edge of human experience and lived to come back and tell the story.

It was Robbie Page who aptly named outside Paumalu (Sunset Beach), DEVIL's GARDEN, the Holy Grail of Extreme Big Wave Surfing.

Eyewitnesses, oceanic scientific data and preponderance of evidence all confirm this monumental achievement, solidifying the Willis brothers place in surfing history.

Their remarkable feat sparked a wave of admiration and inspired a new generation of surfers to push the boundaries of what was once thought impossible in the world of Big Wave Surfing.

If the Willis brothers had surfed these same waves at Nazaré, the Nazare' press machine would be claiming Milton and Michael surfed 250-foot waves and they would have made a statue of them. To quote expert Nazare' big wave surfing champion Garrett MacNamara "...*we're probably riding like 200-footers.*"

Only three people on planet earth have ever been proven to have surfed a 100-foot wave or bigger, Ace Cool at outer Pipeline O'ahu, and Milton Willis and Michael Willis at outer Sunset Beach O'ahu.

In the world of extreme big wave surfing, Ace Cool became chairman of the board, and the world-famous Willis brothers, Milton and Michael, rose to the top and became the current CEOs.

The sacred Kingdom of Hawai'i officially holds the record for the biggest waves ever surfed and remains the number one big wave surfing spot in the world, scientifically supported, backed up by surfers' testimonials, eyewitness accounts, and photo-graphic evidence.

All Glory to the HIGHEST POWER that creates not only 100 FOOT WAVES, but also creates the Power of the entire ocean that resides within each and every one of us.

There is something about being King of the mountain that brings a King to his knees. A Higher Power, Truth, Love and GOD - Generating, Operating, Destroying.

100 times infinite amount of LOVE - Constant and Unconditional.

GLORY to the HIGHEST POWER.

"You were born with wings, why prefer to crawl through life..." - Rumi

In the spirit of Eddie Aikau, the following are the surfers who surfed Sunday, 1/25/98, "Code Black I".

Milton Bradley Willis

Michael Clebert Willis

Ross Clark Jones

Tony Ray

Ted Schmidt

Sven Peltonen

"We are the CHAMPIONS OF THE WORLD" - Freddie Mercury

The following are the surfers who surfed and the surfers who tried on Biggest Wednesday, 1/28/98, "Code Black II".

Milton Bradley Willis

Michael Clebert Willis

Ken Bradshaw

Dan Moore

Cheyne Horan

Sam Hawk

Ross Clark Jones

Tony Ray

Shawn Briley

Ace Cool

Ron Baron

Troy Allotis

Kawika Stant

Noah Johnson

Aaron Lambert

Jason Magers

Greg Russ

Trevor Sifton

Sven Peltonen

DEVIL's GARDEN the Greatest Surfing Story ever told...

100 FOOT WAVE
FREETHINKER ACE COOL
The 'Evel Knievel' of Big Wave Surfing

"Everything is possible with love."
~Michael C. Willis

Alec Cooke, aka Ace Cool, is the first surfer in history to ever be photographed surfing a 100 FOOT WAVE.

It happened in 1985 at outside Pipeline on the North Shore of Oʻahu in the Kingdom of Hawaiʻi. Legendary lensman Warren Bolster was there to capture the historical image from a helicopter. Perhaps the greatest surfing photo ever taken.

Ace Cool was a muscular, bleach blond, larger-than-life character with deep blue eyes. Ace was extremely intelligent and stated he knew every word in the dictionary. When tested he always passed. He wrote a weekly surfing column for the North Shore newspaper about a host of surfing topics from A to Z.

More importantly to his surfing career, Ace was also an off-the-chart waterman. He was able to bodysurf the gnarliest waves 20 feet and higher and was a prolific swimmer.

He said he was a descendant of Captain Cook, the famous naval British explorer, and he claimed to have been a test-tube baby born in 1956.

Ace also had a tremendous sense of humor. When the waves got heavy Ace would be cracking jokes out in the lineup. Big waves did not spook Ace. For him, it was pure FUN!

Ace Cool perhaps the most colorful surfer of all time was quoted as saying, "*I didn't want to be a member of the big wave riders club,*" *I want to be chairman of the board*".

Ace was known as the 'Evel Knievel' of big wave surfing and along with the Willis brothers was voted most likely to die surfing big waves by an Australian surfing magazine.

At night when he wasn't surfing, Ace was a pedicab driver hustling tourists telling them all kinds of stories all the while staying fit and training for his ultimate goal of surfing the biggest wave.

On the day when Ace surfed the historic 100 FOOT wave it was a glorious sunny day in the Kingdom of Hawai'i. The majority of big wave surfers on O'ahu had flown to Maui to surf Honolua Bay knowing that the North Shore would be closed out and un-surfable.

Ace Cool stayed behind. He had other plans to set the record for the biggest wave ever surfed. He first had to commandeer a small private helicopter. So, he hooked-up with lensman Warren Bolster and they hired a pilot that could fly them into the Pacific off-shore trade winds and enable Ace to get past the massive breaking waves and out beyond to outer-reef Pipeline.

After scouring the entire North Shore like a gunslinger searching for the right location Ace directed the pilot to go beyond the outer-reef Pipeline where the waves would be waiting for him.

When they arrived to where the massive waves were thundering in, Ace identified a drop zone where he would make that historic leap of faith into the unknown.

Ace donned an orange wetsuit (rescue orange) so he could be spotted more easily should anything go wrong.

One can only imagine the mixture of excitement and adrenaline Ace was feeling, a real this is it moment.

With all the commitment of marriage "Till death do we part" Ace said "I do" the moment he leapt from the sky bird into the deep blue sea below.

After jumping out of the helicopter, Ace would be all alone in the water. He had no lifeguards, no jet skis, no wave spotters, no life vests, and no fanfare. Only his big wave gun and an overwhelming desire to ride the world's biggest wave.

His big wave gun was his surfboard of choice and of necessity. A surfboard crafted to propel him down the face of massive waves. Pinned shaped nose, single-fin, pin shaped tail, thick, long and wide.

Locked and loaded, Ace then proceeded to paddle himself into a legitimate by all standards 100 FOOT WAVE! The cover page of this book *is the* 100 FOOT WAVE that shows Ace Cool ripping down the face with sheer determination, unmitigated guts, and absolute skill.

The dramatic photograph of Ace Cool made the cover page of the Honolulu Advertiser the very next day. It's doubtful anyone will ever do this again...

The Guinness book of world records possibly unaware of Ace Cool's historic 1985 accomplishment, has credited Sebastian Steudtner of Germany with setting the world record for surfing the biggest wave estimated to be 86 feet.

Traditionally, no one would ever think a German surfer would end up riding the world's biggest wave. After all Germany isn't really known for surfing let alone big waves, but according to the Guinness book of world records and their experts he did.

One of the 'experts' used to determine and confirm Steudtner's Guinness book of world records ride is a University of Southern California associate professor who specializes in geophysical fluid dynamics, Adam Fincham.

Fincham and his team used photographic images and an interview with the two photographers who captured the wave to emerge with the 86 foot wave height.

According to Fincham, to calculate accurately you need the largest ruler possible which often is the jet ski. In the case of Steudtner's wave, there wasn't one positioned correctly within the footage, so they used Steudtner's lower leg as a ruler instead.

Using the Fincham method for determining wave height we can take the 12'0" surfboard that Ace was riding and use it as a ruler. Applying the Fincham method, Ace's 1985 wave is 40 to 60 feet *bigger* than Steudtner's wave in 2020.

Turns out that Ace Cool, not Sebastian Steudtner, is the real-world record holder of the biggest wave ever surfed using photographic evidence and science as proof.

Ace Cool trained a lifetime just to catch that one historic ride which stands the test of time as the all-time biggest wave ever photographed. To accomplish this Herculean feat, Ace spent years honing his skills surfing big waves at Sunset Beach, Pipeline and Waimea Bay.

Contrary and with all due respect, it remains to be seen if Steudtner could even catch a wave at Sunset Beach, Pipeline or Waimea Bay let alone make the drop if he did.

It's a lot easier to summon the courage it takes to challenge big waves when you are surrounded by lifeguards, jet skis, a gallery of wave spotters, and your every move captured on film.

It seems every year, the waves at Nazaré set new world records for the biggest wave ever surfed. We hear of surfers riding 60 and 70 footers as if it were a common occurrence, but when we study the evidence and calculate just how far out Ace Cool was to catch his historic ride, Ace Cool remains the Champion.

Ace's big wave experience, bravery, and training paid off in the most spectacular way possible. Ace accomplished what many once thought impossible and in doing so, officially recognized by the Guinness book of world records or not, Ace Cool cemented his place at the very top of big wave surfing history.

Ace Cool's successful ride on a 100 FOOT wave documented by Warren Bolster in 1985 eviscerates Sebastián Steudtner's and Guinness book of world records claim for the largest waves ever surfed.

The fact that the Guinness book of world records does not officially recognize Ace Cool as the true and legitimate record holder of the biggest waves ever surfed is straight up blasphemy to extreme big wave surfing.

The stone the builder refused is Alec Cooke, aka Ace Cool, the one and only.

The True Ballad of Ace Cool

by Milton and Michael Willis

100 Foot Wave maybe more

The biggest wave that ever came ashore

Way beyond Waimea Bay

The 100 Foot Wave was surfed this Day

They said it cannot be done

Who will be the One?

Who will take the bait?

Who will step up to the plate?

Ace Cool's the One

Ace Cool and his big wave gun

100 Foot Wave maybe more

The biggest wave that ever came to shore

Ace Cool ruled the Day

He schooled the world and paved the way

When he rode a 100 FOOT Wave that day

Now we know the One

Ace Cool and his big wave gun

Chapter 3

Bone-chilling Big Wave Surfing Wipeouts

HOUSE OF PAIN

"If you can't understand the wave you can't respect it. It's only a matter of time before the ocean teaches you to get some."
~Laird Hamilton

When it comes to big wave surfing, there are two times you will always hear the crowd go wild and the volume dramatically increase with yells and screams.

1. For the biggest and best rides.

2. The biggest and worst wipeouts.

Wiping out is an unavoidable part of surfing that every surfer experiences. Generally speaking, most wipeouts are routine and no big deal. However, a wipeout can be a surfer's worst nightmare.

Some of the worst wipeouts in surfing have occurred at Pipeline on the North Shore of O'ahu. Anything can happen there and does. As if the stress of catching a death-defying wave in a packed crowd isn't enough, there is the real threat of hitting the shallow reef or getting stuffed into an Alua hole and never coming out alive.

There also exists the freak factor. The freak factor is when something goes wrong that could not be anticipated, prepared for nor expected.

Beaver Massfeller -

An example of this would be Beaver Massfeller's wipeout on a midsize day at Pipeline. Massfeller, an expert surfer, took off backside on a hollow 8-to-10-foot breaking left. He never made the drop and instead ended up getting pitched by the wave.

Preparing himself for a collision with the hard bottom and the treacherous reef which is primarily made of lava rock and formed coral, Massfeller went into the fetal position and curled up into a little ball.

As he hit the bottom of the wave, the impact forced his knees upward while simultaneously the powerful wave crashing down on him forced his head into his knees. Cracking his head like a walnut.

Massfeller literally caved his own head in and broke his skull. He lived to tell about it and eventually came back to surf some big waves at Sunset Beach, but alas he was never the same surfer.

Michael Willis -

Perhaps next to death, one of the worst tow surfing wipeouts in big waves belongs to Michael Willis.

On a powerful west swell, Michael Willis was tow surfing with his partner, World Champion Surfer Australian Cheyne Horan, at a spot called Phantom's on the North Shore off Velzyland beach.

Michael had just surfed the wave of a lifetime, a 25-to-30-foot barrel all the way across the reef, kicking out just before the wave exploded into a massive close out.

Everything was going perfectly. Horan came charging in to get Michael as they had practiced for months and months. However, what should've been a simple pick up and go became a death trap when Horan in a panic accidently pulled the jet ski's safety lanyard out and the jet ski completely stopped just as tons of ocean was about to come crashing down on them both.

As dangerous as this impending dire situation was, both surfers knew that they could dive through the wave and avoid the explosive impact unscathed. But not so this time.

Both Horan and Michael bailed out to save themselves. Everything went fine for Horan as he was able to get through the wave unscathed.

Michael, on the other hand, had a different kind of fate awaiting him.

As he was diving through the back of the wave the tow rope was sliding against his right thigh. A moment later, the quarter inch braded nylon rope violently cinched itself inextricably around Michael's leg burning through the layers of muscle and flesh down to the bone.

There was no getting out of it. It was a death ride to the beach.

Hopelessly tied to the jet ski and unable to free himself from the rope, Michael was dragged underwater for over a quarter of a mile. It wasn't until the jet ski washed up onto the beach that Michael was able to surface and pull the embedded tow rope from around his leg. Ouch! The rope had cut to the bone, and it was only his knee that kept the rope from filleting Michael's entire leg.

With the aid of another surfer and friend Paul Lyle, Michael was able to make it to his home at Sunset Beach. In shock, he wrapped his leg with gauze, took a Tylenol, drank two beers and went to sleep.

Somehow, perhaps by a miracle despite not receiving any medical treatment or physical therapy, after six weeks Michael was able to fully recover. Michael went on to surf the biggest waves in history a year later "Code Black" 1998, and he is surfing regularly to this today.

David Kahanamoku -

Big wave accidents aren't always caused by the waves. Sometimes it can be other surfers. Such was the case for Hawaiian lifeguard David Kahanamoku, part of Duke Kahanamoku's family tree, who was surfing Waimea Bay on a beautiful northwest day. Northwest days are the easiest and most prime, coveted by those who love surfing Waimea Bay.

With the best waves generally come the most crowds and, on this day, Waimea Bay was thick with surfers. Kahanamoku took off on a wave with several other surfers. Inadvertently, one of the surfers lost his balance causing his surfboard to shoot out and hit Kahanamoku shattering his ankle.

In great pain, Kahanamoku was able to swim in, but he could not manage to get past the powerful 15-foot shorebreak, as in break your neck shore pounding shorebreak. He couldn't stand because of his broken ankle. Unable to get to entirely to the shore safely, Kahanamoku was repeatedly getting swatted like a fly.

Before things got really bad Michael Willis ran into the impact zone picking Kahanamoku up before the next wave would pound him again. Fortunately, lifeguard Derrick Doerner saw what was happening as well and came to assist. Willis and Doerner were able to successfully rescue Kahanamoku and save him from the jaws of death that day.

Taiu Bueno -

Taiu Bueno was one of the greatest big wave surfers from Brazil and in the world. He would regularly challenge huge Sunset Beach and massive Waimea Bay, many times all by himself.

No wave was too big for Bueno.

Turns out it was a wipeout on a small wave that ended Bueno's big wave surfing career.

While surfing at Fernando de Noronha off the northeast coast of Brazil, Bueno pulled into a routine little barrel. He didn't make the wave. Instead, he fell awkwardly, hitting his head on the bottom breaking his neck.

Bueno the Big Wave Champion became quadriplegic and never stood on a surfboard ever again. Today Bueno is back in the ocean surfing with the help of friends and advancements in adapted aquatics.

Wipeouts are not selective. Anyone can have one from the best surfer to the worst surfer at any time on any wave big or small. Perhaps if we learn anything from surfing wipeouts, it's to watch out for one another and be ready to lend aid or a helping hand at a moment's notice.

Surfing and the world itself are better when we all watch out for each other.

Chapter 4

Big Wave Killer Wipeouts

PAYING THE
ULTIMATE PRICE

*"One day I will catch the perfect wave
and keep on riding."*
~Duke Paoa Kahanamoku

Paying the ultimate price –

Surfing big waves is incredibly dangerous, risky, and a thrilling endeavor that requires tremendous skill, courage, and experience. Unfortunately, over the years, many brave big wave surfers have tragically lost their lives while chasing the ultimate thrill.

Robert (Bob) Simmons –

One of the earliest recorded deaths to shock the modern surfing era was Robert (Bob) Simmons who drowned in 1954 while surfing a big day off Windansea beach in La Jolla, California.

Simmons is credited by many for being a master surfboard designer and shaper. He is recognized for being amongst if not the first to use fiberglass and polyester resin to create light weight durable surfboards, a major advancement in surfboard construction.

Simmons had a gimp arm and it is not known exactly how he died while surfing. Possibly his surfboard hit him on his head, or he lost his surfboard during a flurry of waves and was unable to swim in. In the end it doesn't matter how it happened Bob Simmons drowned.

The shallow reef where Simmons drowned a stone's throw away from Windansea is called "Simmons Reef" in honor of Bob Simmons.

Mark Foo –

Perhaps the most well-known of all big wave tragic endings belongs to Mark Foo. Foo was a legendary and popular professional big wave surfer that died while surfing Mavericks, a premiere big wave surf break in Northern California.

In 1994, Foo wiped out on a midsize 15-to-18-foot wave and never resurfaced. For years, no one knew what actually killed Foo. Ultimately, we know now he passed away due to a heart attack. Mark Foo was only 36 years of age.

Donnie Solomon –

Exactly one year to the day that Mark Foo passed, Donnie Solomon died at Waimea Bay on December 23rd, 1995. Solomon had missed catching a wave and instead got caught by the massive wave behind it as he tried to paddle back out to the lineup.

Solomon was thrown over the falls backwards and was pounded fiercely when he landed knocking the air out of his lungs. Cause of death drowning.

Todd Chesser –

As close to perfection as a human can get, Todd Chesser was still human. Extremely handsome, fit, talented and in his prime Chesser tragically died while surfing big waves off the North Shore of Oʻahu.

On February 13th, 1997, a huge swell hit the islands. Chesser and a couple of friends tried paddling out to an outer reef west of Waimea Bay named Alligator Rock. They never made it.

All three were caught inside. Chesser's friends ended up getting washed to shore. Unfortunately, for Todd Chesser he ended up drowning. He was only 28 years old.

Joaquin Miro Quesada –

The first ever surfing fatality at Pipeline on the North Shore of Oʻahu was a South American surfer from Peru, Joaquin Miro Quesada. Miro Quesada came from a wealthy family and was considered a surfing hero in his country for successfully challenging big waves at spots such as La Herradura and Pico Alto.

He met his end in 1967 when he plummeted violently headfirst into the reef at Pipeline on a very big day. Miro Quesada died of blunt force trauma to the head.

Malik Joyeux –

Malik Joyeux an accomplished all-around waterman and expert tube rider from Tahiti died while surfing Pipeline in Hawai'i in 2005. Joyeux was a Tahitian surfing star and a standout at Teahupoo, a notoriously dangerous wave in Tahiti.

After making a steep drop at Pipeline, Joyeux lost his balance at the bottom of the wave and got punished brutally by the full impact of the crest of the wave crashing down on him.

Though he was found 15 minutes later it was too late. Malik Joyeux was just 25 years of age.

Peter Davi –

Renowned big wave surfer Peter Davi died surfing Ghost Tree, Pescadero point off Pebble beach in California. Davi was attempting to surf a huge day. Estimated wave heights by some accounts were 50 to 70 feet.

After losing his surfboard Davi was offered a ride in on a jet ski by a fellow surfer, but he declined. Davi was later found floating face down in the kelp beds. Efforts to revive him were unsuccessful. He was 45 years old.

Sion Milosky –

Sion Milosky was a popular Hawaiian surfer from Kauai who was known for his fearless approach to big wave surfing. In 2011, he tragically died while surfing Mavericks when he wiped out on a massive wave and was held underwater for several minutes. Waves were estimated at 40 to 60 feet.

Unfortunately, no one noticed Sion had not surfaced until approximately 20 minutes later when he was found floating face down. Sion was 35 years old.

Jim Broach –

Jim Broach simply disappeared. On a winter day in Hawai'i 1993 the surf was pumping. Sunset Beach was epic that day and so was the crowd. Experienced big wave surfer Jim Broach elected to pass on Sunset Beach and instead decided to surf a rare, at the time, mysto spot aptly named Phantoms.

Broach was seen paddling out into the massive waves but unfortunately and mysteriously Jim disappeared and was never seen again.

Marcio Freire –

Brazilian "Mad Dog" Freire died while tow surfing waves estimated at 40 to 50 feet in Nazaré along the central coast of Portugal. Marcio Freire was one of the three Brazilian surfers who became known as the "Mad Dogs" after successfully surfing massive waves at Jaws and being featured in the 2016 surfing documentary "Mad Dogs".

Freire was 47 years old and is the first person to die surfing Nazaré.

Mikala Jones –

Mikala Jones was a well-loved, respected father, brother, son, husband, and globally renowned surf star from the North Shore of Oʻahu. Jones grew up surfing the powerful waves of the North Shore including Pipeline, Sunset Beach and Waimea Bay. By the time he was a young man he was already a master surfer on both small and big waves.

To expand his ocean experience, Mikala began traveling in search of discovering perfect waves in exotic and remote locations around the world.

In July of 2023, Mikala was surfing on the other side of the globe in West Sumatra, Indonesia, Mentawai Island chain. Though his expertise and experience in surfing was unsurpassed he tragically died during a freaky accident. Allegedly, either the sharp point at the front of his surfboard or the surfboard's fin cut the inside of his left groin, a wound that was approximately 10 centimeters long. All signs pointed to a severing of the femoral artery.

Cause of death fatal loss of blood. Mikala Jones was 44 years old.

All these surfers were highly skilled and experienced, which shows even the best surfers can and do fall victim to the power of the ocean.

While big wave surfing can be incredibly rewarding, it is important to remember the risks versus the rewards and to keep in mind no matter how much training and preparation a surfer has the ocean will always have Her way.

It's wise to respect all waves big or small.

Experienced surfers know, even the smallest wave has the power of the entire ocean behind it... it's called ultimate RESPECT.

Chapter 5

Hawaiian Big Wave
Surfing Legend Titus Kinimaka

DRAMATIC RESCUE
AT WAIMEA BAY

*"Surfing is about taking risk, that leap of
faith every time I jump in the ocean,
that paddle out among things unseen.
All of these make surfing very special."*
~Shaun Tomson

On a cold Christmas morning in Hawaiʻi, certainly the most dramatic rescue to ever happen in big waves occurred in 1989 at Waimea Bay on the North Shore of Oʻahu.

A powerful 40 foot west swell was hitting Waimea Bay and many of the world's best big wave surfers were out practicing for the upcoming Eddie Aikau Quiksilver big wave surfing contest.

West swell waves at Waimea Bay are the most challenging, notorious for their steepness, power, and difficulty to ride even for the most experienced big wave surfers akin to surfing Backdoor Pipeline on steroids.

Some of the surfing stars out that fateful Christmas day were Ross Clark-Jones, Tony Ray, Milton Willis, Ken Bradshaw, and Louie Ferreira amongst a galaxy of other top riders. But it was Titus Kinimaka who shined the brightest. Kinimaka, the pride of Hawaiʻi was unstoppable, catching every set wave that came through, surfing them as if it was just another day at his home break Kalihiwai on Kauai. It was perhaps one of the greatest surfing performances ever witnessed at Waimea Bay.

Until… taking off impossibly late on an extremely steep wave, Kinimaka shot down the face like a rocket but alas not quite fast enough. A barrel so big you could put a Mack truck inside of it came crashing down squashing Kinimaka onto his surfboard like a flattened bug.

The resulting impact ended up breaking Kinimaka's femur in half. He recalled later while underwater something was hitting him on his head. It turned out it was his foot.

Kinimaka was pummeled, beaten and rag dolled. When he finally came back up to the surface, he let out an anguished scream from the very depths of his soul.

Fortunately for Kinimaka, there were two surfers nearby a young Australian Karl Palmer and Michael Willis.

Risking their lives, Palmer and Willis bravely paddled into the danger zone as fast as they could to rescue Kinimaka. Together the pair hoisted Kinimaka up onto his surfboard and began paddling him into the channel and to safety.

Kinimaka was in great pain, and they didn't want to risk paddling to the beach through the pounding shorebreak. The best they could do to stabilize Kinimaka was to form a human life raft and support him until the rescue helicopter could arrive with twenty-five foot waves exploding around them, and keep Kinimaka from drifting back into the lineup and the XXL pounding waves or even worse getting washed into lava rocks on either side of Waimea Bay.

Making matters more tense were two adult Tiger sharks circling the vicinity. Tiger sharks are known for being aggressive and unpredictable.

By now, most of the surfers in the lineup were aware of the unfolding drama and before long most of the surfers bee-lined for the shore as fast as they could.

Despite the presence of two full grown Tiger sharks, Milton Willis, Robbie Page, and Thierry Vieilledent not thinking of their own personal safety, bravely paddled over to help firm up the edgy situation. At this point Kinimaka's eyes started rolling upward to the back of his head and his teeth began chattering violently. Kinimaka was going into shock.

Having been trained in rescue techniques, Michael knew he had to prevent Kinimaka from going into shock and dying. So, Michael took his wetsuit top off and used his body to give life-saving body heat to Kinimaka, heart to heart.

By now it seemed the entire North Shore community was watching from the shore and the lineup was empty except for Kinimaka and his rescuers.

After what seemed a long 25 minutes or more, Derrick Doerner the lifeguard on duty that day paddled out to see what was going on.

Upon arrival Doerner commanded Willis to get off Kinimaka. "We're *taking him to the beach!*". Willis paid no attention to the order, but instead intently explained to Doerner the dire situation at hand and what needed to be done.

Taking direction from Michael, Doerner radioed for a helicopter, but it would be another long 45 arduous minutes before air support would arrive.

Ken Bradshaw and Louis Ferreira showed up at some point on the scene ostensibly to assist in the rescue.

When the helicopter finally arrived and the Willis brothers were loading Kinimaka into the basket to be airlifted to safety, both Bradshaw and Ferreira were eagerly intent on climbing in it to get out of the danger zone as fast as they could … and they did.

Kinimaka was whisked to the shore where he was transported to the hospital in critical condition.

It would take a few months, but with warrior-like focus and brave-hearted resolve Kinimaka made a full and complete recovery.

Sometime later Kinimaka came to Willis's home at Sunset Beach to thank Michael personally and to say, he could not remember anything about the wipeout, the rescue, nor the helicopter ride.

What Kinimaka *did* remember was Michael's heartbeat and the heat from human touch that saved his life.

The Willis brothers, Milton and Michael along with Karl Palmer, Robbie Paige, and Thierry Vieilledent were unofficially awarded the certificate of life-saving merit from the city and county of Honolulu state of Hawai'i for exhibiting extreme courage and selfless valor during the successful rescue of Titus Kinimaka under extremely hazardous surf conditions. Unsung heroes. True story. Fact.

HAWAIIAN SURFERS ORIGINAL GUARDIANS OF THE SEA

"Semper Paratus ~ Always Ready"
~United States Coast Guard motto

Hawaiian culture is rooted in the love of the sea. Native Hawaiians have a deep connection and understanding of the ocean.

In Hawaiian culture the sea is as important as the land. Way back before anyone ever heard of the term lifeguard, Hawaiian surfers were using the ocean as a source of nourishment, place of worship and also as their favorite playground.

Years before official ocean lifesaving was established Hawaiian surfers had no lifeguards or official training. They didn't need lifeguards because they were the lifeguards. Surfers were apex watermen due to their keen understanding of ocean conditions, currents, and waves.

Hawai'i, the home of the biggest waves ever surfed, is also responsible for the greatest contributions to ocean lifesaving in the world. Real ocean lifesaving as we know it today began and continues to evolve from the Kingdom of Hawai'i.

The term "lifeguard" was likely first popularized in the late 19th century in England, where the duty of watching over swimmers and rescuing those in trouble in the ocean was assigned to specially designated individuals.

In the early 20th century, Wilber E. Longfellow is recognized with organizing America's first lifesaving training program on the East Coast. He is credited with halving the drowning rate at that time.

The concept of lifeguarding has continued to evolve over the years, with the development of formal training programs, standardized rescue techniques, and specialized equipment to aid in water rescues. Today, lifeguards are an essential part of ensuring the safety of people who swim and participate in ocean water-related activities.

In the early 20th century legendary Hawaiian surfer, Olympic swimmer, real lifesaver, and the father of modern surfing Duke Kahanamoku was attributed with introducing the surfboard to lifesaving.

While living in Southern California although not an officially trained lifesaver, on June 14th, 1925, Kahanamoku succeeded in rescuing eight men from a fishing vessel that capsized in heavy surf while it was attempting to enter the city's harbor. Using his surfboard, Kahanamoku made repeated trips from shore to the capsized ship and back.

Before Kahanamoku's heroic rescue lifeguards would usually rely on rowboats or swimming to rescue swimmers in distress. Kahanamoku recognized that he could utilize his surfboard to reach a person in trouble faster and with greater efficiency. He then used the board as a flotation device to transport the person safely back to the shore. This technique transformed the practice of lifeguarding and contributed to the widespread adoption of surfboards used for rescues not just in California and Hawai'i, but also worldwide.

Eddie Aikau teaches the Willis brothers the Hawaiian way to survive rip currents.

In the mid to late sixties the City and County of Honolulu needed a qualified lifeguard to secure the rough wintertime waters of the North Shore on O'ahu.

The man most suited for the job of lifeguarding from Hale'iwa to Sunset Beach was expert big wave surfer Eddie Aikau who became the first lifeguard hired on the North Shore in 1968.

Though Aikau was responsible for patrolling from Hale'iwa to Sunset Beach by himself, no one was ever lost on his watch. For his above and beyond heroism Aikau was named lifeguard of the year in 1971.

It's often said Eddie would go out surfing in the biggest waves when no one else would or could but his contribution to lifesaving is what truly defines his legacy.

Aikau was instrumental in teaching others, specifically surfer's preventative and self-rescue techniques. He warned all to never turn your back on the ocean and cautioned surfers to stay in the waves if they lost their surfboard and had to swim in.

When the surf got big unknowing surfers that lost their surfboards would be tempted to go from the pounding waves to the smooth deep water in the channel where no waves were breaking. Aikau through experience knew the moment a surfer or swimmer got to the channel they would get sucked out to sea and he would be responsible to retrieve them. Preventing a rescue was easier than performing a rescue.

It was Eddy Aikau who schooled future extreme big wave surfing champions the Willis brothers, Milton and Michael, on how to use currents to efficiently get out beyond the breakers and waves to swiftly and safely get back to shore.

The brothers learned well, in 20 plus years of surfing big and small waves in Hawai'i, though both Milton and Michael successfully rescued many they themselves never needed rescuing. Thank you, Hawai'i, Higher Power, and Eddie Aikau.

In 1998 Milton Willis received an official Certificate of Lifesaving Merit for one of his many successful rescues under extremely hazardous conditions from the City and County of Honolulu. Both Milton and Michael are recognized for performing successful rescues on the North Shore during high surf including the historic rescue of Hawaiian big wave surfer and lifeguard Titus Kinimaka at Waimea Bay.

Hanai Hawaiians Milton and Michael teach the world the Hawaiian surfers' way to survive rip currents.

At the beginning of the 21st century, the Willis brothers relocated back to Southern California and set up a very successful school to teach surfing, waterman basics and ocean water safety.

Just as Eddie Aikau had schooled the Willis brothers, Milton and Michael, taught their students respect for the ocean and each other, beginning and advanced surfing techniques and how to avoid and survive rip currents the Hawaiian surfer's way which the students fondly referred to as the Willis way.

Up the beach a few hundred yards from the Willis Brothers Surf School, the City Lifeguards we're running the Jr. Lifeguard program. Occasionally, after camp the kids would get together to finish the day playing in the ocean.

On a late summer afternoon, Jack, one of the Willis brothers' students went swimming with 5 of his friends from the Junior Guard program. They were all between 10 and 12 years old and somewhat accomplished swimmers.

Having a great time, the boys hadn't noticed that they were drifting further and further out. Unbeknownst to them the water was getting deeper and deeper. It was Jack who cautioned the others, "I think we're in a rip current, we better swim to the waves."

The Junior Guard kids scoffed at Jack saying they knew what they were doing. Jack ended up swimming to the waves and getting washed back to shore. As for the Junior Guards, they ended up having to be rescued by the lifeguards.

The very next day Jack couldn't wait to tell all the story. With a huge smile he exclaimed, "I didn't listen to those guys, I knew what to do I swam to the waves the Willis Way! And the waves brought me back to shore just like they said they would!!!"

As fate would have it, later that week with lifeguards on duty at a state beach a few miles north a man and his children drowned after they were caught in a rip current and swept into deep water.

This was epiphany for the Willis brothers. They realized what was common knowledge for experienced Hawaiian surfers was completely foreign to the rest of the world. Avoid rip currents by wading or swimming in front of waves and escape rip currents by going to the waves.

It became the Willis brothers' goal to share this valuable lifesaving information they had learned surfing in the Kingdom of Hawai'i with the rest of the world to help prevent needless drowning and make the ocean safer for all.

They held ocean safety clinics for kids and adults for corporations and the military, wrote articles, made ocean safety videos, and educated the public in every way they could. But their efforts were not enough. They didn't have official clout.

The Willis's began an ambitious campaign to educate and work with the local city and state lifeguards, but the guards were not receptive to the Hawaiian way of surviving rip currents.

Undaunted, Milton and Michael continued undeterred going further up the lifeguard hierarchy reaching out personally to Lifeguard and Fire Captains from San Diego to Los Angeles to no avail.

Exhausting all efforts from the ground up, Milton decided to go to the top by contacting the National Oceanic and Atmospheric Administration (NOAA) and United States Lifeguard Association (USLA) the bodies that dictate and enforce Lifeguard policies.

At first the Hawaiian way to survive rip currents was not well received but due to Milton's persistence it was eventually accepted. USLA personally wrote back

Milton stating that the Willis brothers' input was incorporated into official lifeguard policy as an option to survive rip currents and is posted in pictograph format.

After reading an article that appeared in Ocean Magazine on the Willis brothers and surviving rip currents lifeguard Mike Hutchinson became the first to officially teach the Hawaiian Way of surviving rip currents on the East Coast by including it in Sea Bright New Jersey's Junior Lifeguard program. He called it an extremely valuable "self-rescue" technique for surfers and swimmers alike.

Notwithstanding that the Hawaiian way to avoid and or escape rip currents using waves is now officially adopted by NOAA and USLA many of today's surfers and lifeguards outside of Hawai'i still don't have a clue, more work is needed to make this valuable proven lifesaving information common knowledge.

Lifeguarding from surfboards to jet skis

Today's professional lifeguards have come a long way from Duke's introduction of the surfboard to life saving. Advancements in ocean rescues continue to come directly from Hawai'i. Hawaiian big wave surfer Brian Keaulana revolutionized ocean water safety by being the first to officially utilize the jet ski as an efficient tool to perform swift and or difficult ocean rescues in big and small waves.

Today thanks to Brian Keaulana and other Hawaiian lifeguards every up-to-date lifeguarding program in the world uses jet skis to execute rescues as well as patrol the waters looking for any swimmers in distress or caught in rip currents.

For those who would like to learn more about Hawaii's lifesaving history and its contributions to the world there is a great documentary worth watching written by Jim Kimpton and produced by Marty Hoffman.

Big Wave Guardians' starring big wave surfer and Lifeguard Brian Keaulana which tells the story of Hawaiian lifeguarding and how it is intricately intertwined with surfing and the contemporary culture of Hawai'i.

The importance of Hawai'i and its numerous contributions to the world of surfing, extreme big wave surfing and ocean lifesaving will forever be perpetuated thanks in part to the dedication and efforts of Hawaiian big wave surfers such as Duke Kahanamoku, Eddie Aikau, the Willis brothers Milton and Michael, and Brian Keaulana.

Surviving Rip Currents, the Hawaiian Surfers Way

"Blue out White in"

Eddie Aikau

Big wave surfing legend and Waimea Bay lifeguard Eddie Aikau personally schooled the Willis brothers to become tried, true, and proven Ocean Safety experts.

1. To avoid rip currents, stay in the waves.
2. To escape rip currents, stay calm and swim in the direction of the nearest waves.
3. Never fight the current always flow with the current.
4. Eddie would say *blue out white in.*

In other words, the deep blue calm water is where the rip currents are going out to sea.

The shallower rough white water where the waves are breaking is the ocean water heading to the shore.

The idea is to paddle out with the rip and if you lose your surfboard then swim in with the waves. Stay in the waves to avoid the rip current.

In the spirit of the greatest lifeguard ever to live who is credited with 100's of successful rescues, the Willis brothers continue to honor the life and legacy of Hawaiian big wave surfer Eddie Aikau by sharing with others the Hawaiian Surfers Way to survive rip currents.

"Rips Out, Waves In"
the Willis Brothers

HEAVY WAVE CHAMPIONS OF THE WORLD

*"It's a culmination of your life
when you turn and paddle in
at Mavericks."*
~Jeff Clark

Kingdom of Hawai'i – No ka oi

Big wave surfing was once considered exclusive and practiced only by a handful radical free-thinking individuals mostly in Hawai'i.

Currently, big wave surfing is a global phenomenon. There are big waves being discovered all over the world from Indonesia to Ireland to Chile to Alaska, and everywhere in between. Today the world is fascinated with big wave surfing.

The Kingdom of Hawai'i is the home of big wave surfing and until recently was considered the Mecca for all big wave surfers wanting to experience the thrill of surfing big waves and make a name for themselves.

Mavericks, California -

This all changed with the discovery of Mavericks in Northern California. Before a surfer named Jeff Clark who shared with the surfing world photographs of towering waves south of San Francisco most surfers thought California had no big waves.

Turns out some of the most rideable and dangerous big waves in the world are located off California and Baja California.

Clark became an international celebrity and legendary surfer when he introduced Mavericks to the surfing world in 1990. California was now considered a premier big wave location.

In time, expert big wave surfers such as Ken Bradshaw, Mark Foo, Garrett McNamara, and others began going from Hawai'i to California to chase down these massive waves.

This was a major shift marking the first time that surfers were gaining legendary status in the world of big wave surfing somewhere other than Hawai'i.

And as it turns out, not too much time later Mark Foo became the first surfer who tragically lost his life at Mavericks. This only made Maverick's reputation as a big wave more notorious.

Now Mavericks was a killer.

Todos Santos Island, Baja California -

In the late 1980's, professional surfers Tom Curran and Dave Parmenter were filmed surfing big waves off Todos Santos Island which is located 10 miles off the coast of Ensenada in Baja California Norte. And in 1998, Taylor Knox from Carlsbad California put Todos Santos solidly on the big wave surfing map with a ride estimated to be over 50 feet.

For his incredible efforts, Knox received international acclaim, winning the K2 XXL Big Wave Challenge and

$50,000 prize money for the biggest wave surfed that year.

This was the same year Hawai'i had its first ever "Code Black" and the Willis brothers, Milton and Michael, surfed it. Although there were dramatic pictures of the Willis brothers paddling into huge "Code Black" Waimea Bay, the winner went to Taylor Knox.

Surfing magazine said the Willis brothers were "the *unofficial winners*" of the K2 Big Wave contest.

Cortez Banks, California -

In 2001, another big wave surfing spot was discovered 100 miles or so off the coast of California, the Cortez Banks. Professional surfers Mike Parsons, Peter Mel and Brad Gerlach were filmed surfing waves estimated to be 50 feet plus.

Parsons was credited with surfing a wave over 65 feet resulting in the Guinness book of world records for largest wave ever surfed and prize money of over $50,000. It's safe to say the world of big wave surfing was now wide open.

Dungeons, South Africa –

Dungeons, a big wave surfing spot located near Cape Town, South Africa is known to have been surfed in the 80's and is regarded by many to be the counterpart to Mavericks in California.

The waves at Dungeons are created by a deep underwater canyon and can reach heights of over 50 feet.

Some of the most famous big wave surfers associated with Dungeons include Grant "Twiggy" Baker, who has won multiple contests at the break, and Chris Bertish, who famously paddled into a massive wave in 2010.

Nazaré, Portugal -

In 2011, 44-year-old big wave surfer Garrett McNamara from Hawai'i claimed to have surfed a wave in Nazaré estimated at over 75 feet high.

Suddenly, the Kingdom of Hawai'i, home of extreme big wave surfing was now regulated to second best. Nazaré was being hailed as the world's largest rideable waves and the Guinness book of world record was now theirs.

The beauty of Nazaré is the photographic angle often associated with it which makes the waves look much bigger than the waves actually are.

What the Guinness book of world records was calling a 78 foot wave in Nazaré is considered 35 to 40 foot wave tops in Hawai'i.

Currently, Sebastian Steudtner from Germany, holds the official Guinness book of world records for biggest wave ever surfed at Nazaré in October 2020 making

Nazaré allegedly the home for biggest waves in the world.

Are you ready for this? Nazaré has the biggest waves ever surfed in the world is in reality the biggest hype ever in the surfing world.

Kingdom of Hawai'i -

What the Guinness book of world records, McNamara and Steudtnar do not acknowledge is that Alec Cooke, aka Ace Cool, was documented surfing a 100 FOOT WAVE at outer reef Pipeline in 1985.

As well in 1998, the Willis brothers along with Ken Bradshaw were documented surfing waves at Outer Log Cabins estimated at 85 to 90 feet. This was back in 1998!

Many qualified surfing experts apart from Guinness book of world records point to 1/28/98 in the Kingdom of Hawai'i as the biggest waves ever surfed bar none.

After surfing Outer Log Cabins, the Willis brothers ventured to DEVIL's GARDEN another half a mile to a mile out encountering waves estimated to be consistently well over 100 feet. Fact.

On the scene this monuMENTAL day photographer Hank Foto stated,

"I saw 100 FOOT WAVEs that were so Big they looked fake!"

Those who truly care about truth and accuracy will do the homework. After checking storm data, swell heights, wave intervals and other pertinent information the results confirm…

The biggest waves in the world are found and surfed in the Kingdom of Hawai'i.

Chapter 8

Small Waves, Big Waves, Extreme Big Waves

HOW TO MEASURE WAVES

"Even the smallest wave has the power
of the entire ocean behind it."
~Michael Clebert Willis

Ever wonder how waves are measured?

From the beginning, waves were measured by juxtaposition using the surfer's body in ratio to the face of a wave. Identifying waves as flat and going up from there to ankle high, knee high, waist high, shoulder high, head high, overhead high, double overhead triple, quadruple, five times overhead, and after that almost incomprehensible.

Live visual observations are the most basic and oldest method of wave measurement. It involves simply looking at the waves and estimating their height and period. This method is the standard widely used today.

The problem with eyewitness observation is unless there is some kind of reference point such as a surfer on the wave, it is extremely difficult to estimate wave heights even for the most experienced surfers.

Big waves appear small in the distance. It's not uncommon for surfers to see 'small' waves afar, only to paddle out and find the small waves they saw were in reality substantially bigger than first thought.

While photographs can be impressive, they are not a scientific method for accurately measuring waves.

Ever since John Severson founded Surfer magazine in 1962, the world's first surfing magazine, surfers have used photographic images as a way to measure wave heights.

The problem with using photographs as evidence to measure wave heights is that photographs don't always tell the entire picture. To get the most impact out of his visual images Severson employed the photography trick of tilting the photo and changing its angle so that he could make a 10 foot wave look 30 feet.

It turns out photographic angles can and do radically change one's perception of just how big or small a wave actually is. The very same wave filmed from different angels makes a world of difference. A 5 foot wave filmed from a higher angle can easily appear 25 feet or bigger.

Most people would be surprised to find out Sebastian Steudtner's Guinness book of world records for surfing the world's largest wave is based off of a photograph and a few guys behind closed doors in a dark room using Steudtner's lower leg in the photo as a measurement reference. Where is the actual science backing Steudtner's claim up?

In truth, Guinness Book of World Records for surfing the world's largest wave is based more on hype and sensationalism rather than science and fact and is tainted by need/greed and monetary motivations.

The sensationalism and hype surrounding the big wave spot Nazaré is a perfect example of this. Waves that would be considered 35 feet in the Kingdom of Hawai'i are dubbed 78 feet plus in the Portugal town of Nazaré. And why not, it's good for business.

It must be acknowledged that the photographs of Nazaré waves are nothing short of spectacular. Photographers go to great lengths to get just the right angle.

The right angle being the one that makes the wave look its very biggest. In this case it really doesn't matter how big or small a wave may actually be. What matters and pays is how big a wave appears to be in the media.

Photographic evidence for measuring wave heights is in reality no evidence at all. Real evidence comes down to science, numbers, and hard facts, not a photo and some guy in a room measuring with a ruler.

After analyzing the science, it turns out the Kingdom of Hawai'i has the biggest waves in the world. Nazaré is to be respected for sure, but it is not in the same league as Hawai'i.

Before Nazare' became famous for having the world's largest waves and a booming economy thriving off tourists and rich surfers dollars it was a sleepy, impoverished little beach community. Follow the money.

The following are some of the scientific methods used to measure waves today.

Wave buoys. Wave buoys are instruments that measure the height, period, and direction of ocean waves. They are anchored to the seafloor and transmit data to shore via satellite. Wave buoys are widely used for oceanographic research, wave monitoring, and tsunami warning systems.

Pressure sensors. Pressure sensors are devices that measure changes in water pressure caused by passing waves. They are often used in combination with wave buoys and can provide accurate measurements of wave height and period.

Acoustic Doppler Current Profiler (ADCP). ADCP are instruments that use sound waves to measure water currents and wave characteristics. They can measure wave height, period, and direction as well as water velocity and direction. ADCPs are widely used in oceanographic research and wave monitoring.

Remote sensing. Remote sensing involves using satellites and radar to measure waves from outer space. This method can provide a broad-scale view of wave patterns across large areas of the ocean and is often used for weather forecasting and oceanographic research.

Lidar. Lidar, which stands for Light Detection and Ranging, is a laser-based technology that can measure the height and shape of waves. It works by bouncing laser beams off the ocean surface and measuring the time it takes for the beams to return. Lidar is still a relatively new technology, but it has the potential to provide accurate, high-resolution measurements of waves in real-time.

Perhaps the most accurate way to measure waves comes from legendary big wave surfer Buzzy Trent relating how waves can be measured … *"in increments of fear."*

Truth be told, the first time you witness a 100 FOOT WAVE up close face to face you won't see a 100 FOOT WAVE you will see GOD.

BIG WAVE SURFING
& BIRTH OF EXTREME
BIG WAVE SURFING

*"Follow your heart and
fear does not exist."*

~Garrett McNamara

Trust and believe that there is no such thing as half-heartedness when it comes to surfing the biggest waves. It's 100 % *"Go Go Go"* no turning back full-hearted commitment.

Setting the stage -

Big wave surfing has become a subculture within the broader surfing world. The scene surrounding it emphasizes physical fitness, mental toughness, and a willingness to take bold risks.

The gallant and audacious surfers who pursue big wave riding are amongst the most passionate and committed athletes in the world.

Early 20ᵗʰ Century -

In the 20th century, surfing was a fringe sport that was practiced primarily by native Hawaiians. Duke Paoa Kahanamoku is considered the father of modern-day surfing for his contributions to surfing and ocean lifesaving.

In 1917, Kahanamoku was witnessed catching a huge wave with a long, heavy wooden surfboard and riding it for over a mile. He personally estimated the wave to be 30 feet high.

In the 1950's, a handful of adventurous surfers began exploring the outer limits of what was possible on a surfboard. They started to ride waves that were twice as big as the standard waves that most surfers were accustomed to.

Early big wave surfing pioneers began to push the boundaries of big wave surfing at renowned spots such as Makaha located on the west side of Oʻahu and later at Sunset Beach and Waimea Bay on the North Shore.

Some of the first notable big wave surfers included Greg Noll, Fred Van Dyke, George Downing, Buzzy Trent, Pat Curren, Wally Froiseth and Peter Cole.

Mid-20th Century –

In the 1980's, surfers like Mark Foo, Ace Cool, James Jones, and Keone Downing pushed the limits of big wave surfing even further by challenging the outer reefs previously thought impossible to surf.

Intrepid female surfers such as Joyce Hoffman, Margo Oberg, Debbie Beecham, and Betty Depolito were instrumental trailblazers of big wave surfing in the 80's and 90's and they helped lay down the foundation for today's women extreme big wave surfers.

Late 20th Century - A REAL GAME CHANGER!

The biggest waves ever surfed in the 20th century to the present.

In 1985, Ace Cool whose real name is Alec Cooke became the first surfer ever documented surfing a

100 FOOT WAVE! Historic Photo by Warren Bolster.

The mid to late 1990's saw the rise of tow-in surfing. A method where an external force, such as jet ski or a motorboat would tow surfers into waves that were previously considered un-surfable. This allowed surfers to take on even bigger waves.

Names such as Buzzy Kerbox, Laird Hamilton, Milton Willis, Michael Willis, Dave Kalama, and Ken Bradshaw became synonymous with extreme big wave tow-in surfing.

In 1998, the Willis brothers Milton and Michael joined Alec Cooke as the only 3 people in history proven to have surfed waves 100 feet or more when they were documented surfing Outer Log Cabins. And a mile further out credited with surfing waves well in excess of 100 feet at DEVIL's GARDEN, outside Sunset Beach.

The New Millenium -

In the 21st century, big wave surfers now understand that there are no limits on the size of waves that surfers can and do ride.

For today's extreme big wave surfers, the allure of the 100 FOOT WAVE constantly looms on the horizon. It is the eagerly sought after Holy Grail of Extreme Big

Wave Surfing. Surfers, figuratively and literally, are prepared and do sacrifice their lives in pursuit of it.

What drives these individuals to lay their lives on the line for a 100 FOOT WAVE? Is it the pursuit of happiness, the ultimate thrill, a death wish, fortune and fame? Unification with the universe and eternal life?

The truth is 100 FOOT WAVES are very rare indeed and surfing a 100 FOOT WAVE is beyond anything that yesterday's big wave surfers ever imagined. But alas, we know now it's not only possible, it's been done by a few surfers that you can count on one hand Ace Cool, Michael Willis and Milton Willis.

For comparison, more people have been to the moon than have surfed a *100 FOOT WAVE!*

◆◆◆

BIG WAVE SURFING LEGEND
MARK FOO

"Eddie would Go."
~Mark Foo

In the winter of 1978/79, Mark Foo was a rising superstar living on the South Shore of Oʻahu. Michael Willis was living and working shaping surfboards on Holawa Street at Sunset Beach on the North Shore. By chance, or fate, Foo was looking for a shaper for his new line of surfboards called Hawaiian Vibrations by Mark Foo.

It was Ed Searfoss who glassed basically 80% of all the surfboards on the North Shore who made the connection between Foo and Willis.

Mark Foo was surfing on the International Professional Surfing (IPS) tour at the time and would come see Michael to work on Hawaiian Vibrations and his personal small wave surfboards for the upcoming Australian leg of the tour.

Because Michael lived just a few hundred yards from the waves it was a great place to go surf and rinse the dust off after shaping.

Inevitably, Foo joined Willis and they began surfing Sunset Beach regularly together. At this time, both surfers encouraged each other to take off on bigger and bigger waves steeper and deeper each time.

Foo's surf contest results were somewhat lackluster on the professional tour. He was getting great exposure, cover shots, centerfolds and so on, but couldn't seem to rise upward in the small wave competitive arena. To continue being a professional surfer there was only one way for Foo to go and that was into the world of big wave surfing which meant Waimea Bay at the time.

This was an exciting period for big wave surfing, as leashes had never been used before in waves 20 feet and above. Mark Foo was amongst the very first surfers to use a leash at Waimea Bay on a big swell.

Around the same time, Simon Anderson, an Australian professional surfer and highly sought after surfboard shaper and designer, had just introduced the three-fin design for small wave surfboards to the surfing world to compete with the twin fin design that Australian professional surfer and 4x World Champion, Mark Richards had designed with Hawaiian Reno Abellera and was winning all the contests with.

Foo and Willis began working on 3-fin designs for big waves which turned out to be a major breakthrough for big wave surfboards at the time.

Mark Foo was the first to ride a 3-fin surfboard in waves over 25 feet, 50 feet by today's standards.

Up until this time, Foo was primarily known as a small wave surfer and now he was a rising star headed toward the top of the big wave pecking order with the likes of fellow big wave surfers James Booby Jones, Ken Bradshaw, Ace Cool and Peter Cole.

Foo became known as one of the most brave and skilled big wave surfers in the world.

Overtime, Waimea Bay was no longer the only game in town for big wave surfing.

Foo was amongst the first to "chase" extreme big swells flying to Maverick's in California, Todos Santos in Mexico, and Pico Alto in Peru. Surfing magazine published a centerfold of Foo surfing on a Milton Willis shape at huge Todos Santos.

Mark Foo was a gun slinger with the kind of gun that surfs big waves, have guns will travel… for money.

Tragically however, on December 23rd, 1994, Mark Foo lost his life surfing mid-sized waves at Mavericks in Half Moon Bay.

Killer wipeouts are one hell of a price to get your fix.

While one would think that seeing one of the world's best big wave surfer's lose his life surfing would detour others from taking up the challenge of big wave surfing, it's been just the opposite.

Big wave surfing is more popular than ever. It seems nowadays everybody including their brother, sister, daughter, and son wants to become a big wave surfer. And if they don't want to be a big wave surfer then they want to watch the big wave surfers perform.

Mark Foo was successful, charismatic, handsome, and intelligent. He was the perfect front man to promote big wave surfing.

Foo as much as anybody before or after him has played a pivotal part in big wave surfing's development.

Mark Foo can be credited with being the augur to Extreme Big Wave Surfing.

Surfing Big Waves to Extreme Big Waves

BEGINNING OF THE TOW SURFING ERA

"Surfing is almost a way to fly."
~Jeff Hackman

The late 1990's marked a turning point in big wave surfing with the advent of tow surfing.

Tow surfing, also known as "tow-in" surfing, is a technique where a surfer is towed into a wave by a jet ski or other motorized watercraft, allowing them to catch waves that are too big and too fast to paddle into. Tow surfing opened the doors to Extreme Big Wave surfing.

The origins of modern tow surfing can be traced back to the Hawaiian big wave surfer Buzzy Kerbox and his friend and tow partner, Laird Hamilton.

In the mid-1990's, Kerbox and Hamilton began experimenting with using a motorized zodiac to tow each other into late winter and early spring waves.

While Sunset Beach and other big wave spots were crowded with surfers, further outside Kerbox and Hamilton had the outside reefs all to themselves.

It was Buzzy Kerbox and his zodiac that initiated the modern tow surfing movement.

After seeing Kerbox and Hamilton tow surfing Milton Willis and Ken Bradshaw were the first to try high powered jet skis on the North Shore.

During this time there were no official regulations or training programs established. Milton had to develop his own tow in and rescue techniques that are still being used today.

At first, tow surfing was resisted among most big wave surfers. Under Milton Willis's mentorship big wave surfers such as Cheyne Horan, Tony Ray and Ross Clark-Jones and others began to embrace and practice tow in surfing.

It would be 4 to 5 years before tow surfing would become the standard norm for extreme big wave surfing.

During the nascent years of tow surfing the outside reefs were wide open and empty.

The only tow-in teams to regularly surf the outside reefs on the North shore were Milton Willis and Cheyne Horan, Michael Willis and Robbie Page, Ken Bradshaw and Dan Moore, Ace Cool and Ron Barren, and Laird Hamilton and Derrick Doerner who would come out occasionally, but they mostly were concentrating on a spot in Maui called Jaws.

Like any new endeavor, tow surfing was all trial and error.

- How big or little should the surfboard be for optimum performance?
- Would a weighted surfboard perform better?
- Should there be straps to lock in a surfer's feet, or not?

And safety equipment... there was none.

No safety vest to employ should trouble arise nor safety sleds to pick up a surfer quickly and efficiently after a ride.

One of the first outings for the Willis brothers almost ended in disaster.

On a cool crisp early morning, Milton and Michael were tow surfing with Laird Hamilton and Derrick Doerner in waves estimated by today's standards as big as 50 to 60 feet plus. Waimea Bay was closed out and except for these two teams no one else was out that day.

Powerful waves were breaking out as far as the eyes could see. Waves were approaching at approximately 25 second intervals. Nonstop extreme big waves one after the other steamrolling in. Hamilton and Doerner were able to make it out safely. The Willis brothers were not as fortunate.

After going out to what seemed a mile or more, the brothers were less than 500 yards from making it safely outside. Milton was towing Michael when a monster rogue wave exploded right in front of them.

Milton abruptly button hooked the jet ski and gunned it for the shore and to safety.

Unfortunately for Michael when Milton abruptly turned the jet ski around, he did it in such a way that the tow rope went slack and Michael was left with no choice but to go prone. As Milton hit the throttle full blast, the tow rope was jerked hard, and it was all that Michael could do but to hold on for dear life.

At first, it seemed they would be able to outrun the monster wave chasing them down. The only problem… Milton was racing so fast that Michael was now violently bouncing 5 feet up into the air and slapping back down hard like a skipping stone.

Not wanting to slow Milton down and knowing he would be bucked off any second, Michael let go of the rope. The last thing Michael saw before turning around to face the music was Milton going 40 miles an hour as fast as he could to shore.

Despite years of big wave training, Michael had never been this far out in waves this big before. At this point, all he could do is face the wave and dive as deep as possible before being impacted which he did.

It's an eerie feeling being all alone half a mile out or more in deep dark water where the wild things are and hearing 50 foot waves rumbling overhead with more like it coming in right behind.

Michael thought he was prepared for what came next. He had a big wave disaster procedure to follow. He would dive down feet first, keeping his eyes wide open looking for bubbles going shoreward to grab on, to stay present, stay calm, and keep praying.

Timing it perfectly, Michael Willis was able to negotiate the first wave. Despite the explosive beating, amazingly the surfboard leash Michael was using did not break. But now it was stretched to a 30 foot leash the diameter of a thin string.

Michael abandoned the leash and ditched his surfboard shoving it to the side just before diving under the next big wave.

Upon resurfacing, Michael had to clear a space through the thick layer of sea foam up to six feet thick to get a valuable lifesaving breath of air before diving back down feet first just before the next wave detonated.

Michael kept his eyes open underwater looking for the turbulent bubbles that would lead him to shore.

The entire ordeal of diving, getting dragged, resurfacing, clearing the layers of sea foam, over and over again would take Michael approximately 45 minutes to get back to shore half the time swimming and half getting washed back in with the waves.

Back at the beach, there was an alarmed woman on the phone with the Coast Guard calling for help. She had seen Michael's surfboard washed up on the beach with no swimmer in sight. Both the woman and Milton had been frantically looking for Michael and were thankful to God when they saw he had made it back to the shore safe and alive.

Despite the severity of the situation Hamilton and Doerner had just kept on surfing.

Later, Doerner related that he and Hamilton had been looking for Michael on the outside. Doerner added if that happens again the best thing is to swim out another quarter mile through the massive waves to the open ocean.

Truth be told, it would have been humanly impossible to do that for anyone, even for the great Laird Hamilton.

Since those early times tow in surfing has advanced leaps and bounds. Safety equipment has evolved to include inflatable vests, safety sleds and new rescue techniques that help make tow surfing as safe as it can be.

It also helps to know most times nowadays there will be multiple tow teams out to help watch out for one another.

These were the days of early tow surfing, pure and uncharted. Today the road has been mapped out and paved. These big wave surfers Buzzy Kerbox, Laird Hamilton, Ken Bradshaw, Milton Willis, Michael Willis and Ace Cool are credited for pioneering extreme big tow surfing. Fact.

Big Wave Surfing
NOW, MIND/BODY, BODY/MIND UNIFICATION

"Fear causes hesitation and hesitation will cause your worst fears to come true."

~Patrick Swayze

Riding a 100 FOOT WAVE is not for the faint of heart.

It requires 100% commitment, supernatural mental fortitude, and supreme physical endurance.

The body works best when it works with the mind and the mind works best when it works with the body. This is called mind and body unification.

There are many different types of training that surfers use to get their bodies and minds ready to surf big waves.

Physical Training -

Big wave surfers need to be in peak physical condition to surf waves that can reach heights of 100 feet or more. They must have strong core muscles to maintain balance and stability on their boards, powerful leg muscles to generate speed and control, and excellent cardiovascular fitness to endure the physical exertion of paddling and riding the waves.

Many big wave surfers engage in a variety of physical training activities to prepare themselves for the challenges of surfing massive waves. These include weightlifting, swimming, running, yoga, and other forms of exercise that improve strength, flexibility, and endurance.

There are surfers that like to use the gym or employ specially designed workouts for strength and breath training.

The most natural and common way surfers train for big waves is the waterman basics swimming, running, paddling and free diving.

More serious surfers take their gym underwater to practice free diving at the bottom of the ocean picking up a heavy rock and running with it.

There are two thoughts about this. One is that by holding your breath and running underwater with a heavy rock that stamina and endurance are increased better preparing a surfer for long hold downs after bad wipeouts.

The other thought is it's better to dive down and relax for as long as possible with the goal of slowing your heart and mind down making it easier to stay submerged longer by keeping relaxed physically and mentally.

Mental Training -

Surfing big waves is a dangerous, high risk, unpredictable activity and surfers must be mentally prepared to handle whatever challenges come their way.

In addition to physical training, big wave surfers must also train their minds to stay focused and stay calm under extreme pressure.

This can involve visualization exercises, meditation, breathing techniques, and other mental training practices that help surfers manage their fear, anxiety, and stress during extremely precarious situations.

The mind of a big wave surfer has to be 100% positive. There can be no room for doubt. Confidence is a big wave surfer's best friend; doubt is their worst enemy.

It's never can I make it, or will I make it, it's always I *am* making it no matter what the odds are.

It's wholehearted full commitment 100% *"Go Go Go"*.

To work optimally, the body and the mind must be relaxed and in harmony. There's a technique that experienced highly aware big wave surfers have learned to coordinate their mind and their body.

Generally speaking, when the mind becomes tense due to the situation, the body will also become tense. The trick is when you feel your mind tensing up try to relax your body even if it's just your baby finger and as your body relaxes your mind will also.

Relax the mind to have a relaxed body.

Relax the body to have a relaxed mind.

<u>**Spiritual Training**</u> -

Many big wave surfers describe surfing as a spiritual experience, one that unifies them to something larger than themselves and helps them feel more alive and present in the moment.

Big wave surfers must stay connected to the ocean and the waves they are riding on a spiritual level.

This can involve developing a deep respect and reverence for the natural world and cultivating a sense of humility and gratitude for the opportunity to surf such magnificent waves.

By cultivating a spiritual connection to the ocean and the waves, surfers can tap into a deeper source of strength and inspiration that can help them overcome even the most daunting of challenges.

The training techniques above are an essential part of preparing to surf big waves. Big wave surfers must train their bodies, minds, and spirits to handle the physical, mental, and spiritual demands of the sport. By doing so, they can increase their chances of success and develop a deeper appreciation for the beauty and power of the ocean.

In the NOW –

The final crucial element for big wave surfing is the ability for an individual to be in the *NOW*, the fourth realm of training. When taking off on a big wave a surfer cannot afford to be thinking about anything except for the present moment and then dealing with it as it presents itself.

It's in this _NOW_ moment that humans feel most alive and operate at their best.

Many surfers describe big wave surfing as a sensual or metaphysical experience beyond one that is physical or mental, one that connects them to something larger than themselves that helps them feel more alive and present in the moment. A real sense of belonging to something much grander than the wave, the power behind the wave.

One does not have to be a big wave surfer to understand the unlimited benefits of living one hundred percent in the present moment.

Everything happens in the _NOW_. When we approach life with wholehearted commitment, dealing with it in the _NOW_, our chances of success in any endeavor are significantly increased.

Big Wave Surfing
INTREPID WAHINE's

*"Being creative on a wave is
challenging, but we each create
art in our own way."*
~Bethany Hamilton

Big wave surfing was once considered a male-dominated sport, but over the years, women have broken through barriers and proved their skill and bravery on the biggest waves on the planet. In this chapter, we will take a closer look at some of the past and present day best big wave women surfers and their accomplishments.

It's important to remember women have excelled at big wave surfing since the very beginning. In ancient Hawai'i, women surfers were considered equal to male surfers and were highly respected for their surfing abilities. In fact, surfing was a popular sport among both men and women in ancient Hawai'i, and it was not uncommon for women to surf alongside men.

There are many stories and legends throughout Hawaiian culture that highlight the skill and bravery of female surfers. For example, there is the legend about a Hawaiian princess named Kelea who was a skilled surfer and traveled from island to island to surf the best waves.

Another legend tells the story of a woman named La'ieikawai who surfed a massive wave and was carried inland by the force of the wave.

In ancient Hawai'i, surfing was not just a sport, but also a way of life and a means of connecting with the ocean and the spiritual world. Women surfers were respected for their connection to the ocean and their ability to ride the waves with grace and skill.

Overall, in ancient Hawai'i, surfing was an important part of their culture, practiced by both men and women. Women were celebrated for their surfing abilities as it should be.

"Banzai Betty" -

Betty Depolito originally from Florida maybe the first woman to seriously focus on surfing big waves. Her nickname was "Banzai Betty" earned for her stand out performances in wild and dangerous surf at Pipeline on the North Shore of O'ahu.

Depolito also pushed the limits of women's surfing by regularly riding big waves at Sunset Beach as well as huge Waimea Bay. For many years, Depolito would be the only woman out charging in a male dominated lineup.

The very first big wave surfing contest exclusively held for women was founded in 2010 by the one and only "Banzai Betty" Depolito.

Depolito established the Woman's Waimea Bay Championship Big Wave contest specifically for women to be held in some of the biggest most dangerous waves in the world.

Depolito's big wave surfing contest pays respect to powerful free-thinking women who have worked tirelessly to open doors previously locked shut.

Women get to have a day where they can really highlight and showcase their skills and abilities in heavy surf conditions.

Today, the contest is called "Queen of the Bay" and indeed younger girls interested in big wave surfing now have something they can aspire to become one day, the Queen of the big waves.

It's safe to say that "Banzai Betty" Depolito opened the door for many big wave female surfers and today women can be seen surfing right alongside the men in the largest of waves.

Emi Erickson -

Emi Erickson is a regular in big waves, especially at Waimea Bay and Sunset Beach in Hawai'i, her home base. She learned from the best, her father Rodger Erickson, a legendary big wave surfer in his time.

Emi is an accomplished and graceful surfer who turns heads with her big wave performances highlighting feminine athleticism at its finest.

Maya Gabeira -

Maya Gabeira, originally from Brazil, is the woman surfer that holds the current Guinness book of world record for the largest wave ever surfed. In 2018, she rode a massive 68 foot wave at Nazaré Portugal, breaking her own previous record of 62 feet.

Gabeira is the first woman known to surf Nazaré back in 2011 and continues to push the boundaries of big wave surfing for women.

It should be noted that Gabeira is also one of the highest paid professional surfers in the world man or woman.

Paige Alms -

Paige Alms was born in Canada. But as fate had it grew up in Hawai'i. She is a credited with being amongst the first women surfers to charge some of the biggest surf at Jaws, aka Pe'ahi Maui.

Jaws is at the top of the list when it comes to dangerous big wave surfing spots and to witness Alms taking on these extremely big waves is nothing short of spectacular.

Alms has won multiple Big Wave Awards, including the Women's Best Overall Performance award in 2016 and again in 2017. One can't help but be impressed to see this beautiful lady competing side by side with the guys for the biggest waves in the world.

Justine Dupont -

One of today's greatest big wave surfers is Justine Dupont a French surfer who has been surfing big waves since she was just a teenager.

In 2013, Dupont became the very first woman to surf waves upwards of 50 feet at Belharra in the Northern Basque Country of France. In 2020, she won the prestigious first ever Nazaré Tow-In Challenge and made history yet again in 2021 by becoming the first woman to surf a wave estimated over 70 feet at Nazaré, Portugal.

Dupont has repeatedly shattered many barriers by surfing the biggest waves in the world by any man or woman.

Bethany Hamilton -

Bethany Hamilton from the island of Kaua'i, who lost her arm in a shark attack at 13 years of age, may be perhaps the most inspirational big wave surfer of all, male or female. Bethany has charged huge waves at Jaws, also known as Pe'ahi, paddled into ferocious waves at Pipeline and gotten barreled all with just one arm. Many surfers with two arms would find the waves Bethany rides more than challenging. Big respect "Hoihi" for the girl from Kaua'i, an inspiration of inner strength and beauty for overcoming difficult obstacles and challenges. She credits God.

"Banzai Betty" Depolito, Maya Gabeira, Justine Dupont, Bethany Hamilton, and many other outstanding women big wave riders have come a long way proving that gender is no barrier to riding the biggest waves in the world. They have pushed the limits of what is possible and have inspired a new generation of female surfers to follow in their footsteps. Major RESPECT.

Chapter 14

North Shore of Oahu Surfboard Craftsman
THE 'GO-TO MAN'
ED SEARFOSS

*"The three most important things
in life...Surf, Surf, Surf."*
~Jack O'Neill

In the world of surfing, perhaps no one has glassed more big wave surfboards than Ed Searfoss.

Searfoss has been glassing surfboards big and small on the North Shore of Oʻahu for 50 years and is considered the "go to guy" when a surfboard needs to be glassed literally overnight for an upcoming big swell or important surfing contest.

Between the mid 1980's and the year 2000, the Willis brother's surfboards dominated on the North Shore especially at Sunset Beach, Pipeline and Waimea Bay. Ed Searfoss is the main man responsible for glassing 90% of the surfboards the Willis brothers were shaping during this time period.

The list of surfers who have relied on the Willis brothers to shape and Ed Searfoss to glass their surfboards reads like a Who's Who with the likes of legendary surfers such as Mark Foo, Titus Kinimaka, Ace Cool, Liam McNamara, Garrett McNamara, Jason Magers, Andy and Bruce Irons, and many more.

In addition to glassing some of the best big wave guns ever created, Searfoss was instrumental in helping to design the tow-in surfboards for extreme big waves.

When it came to experimenting with weight, Searfoss would chamber out specific areas on the deck of the surfboard and fill it back up with a carefully weighted amount of BB's and then reseal it. A Willis brothers tow surfboard glassed by Searfoss with added BBs for weight was used in 1998 during "Biggest Wednesday" and is now in California at the Oceanside surfing museum.

Searfoss a practical man always had a solution to any problems that would come up while glassing a surfboard. If a surfboard's rocker was too much or not enough, he would simply put a brick or two on it during lamination reducing or increasing the rocker to his discernment. There isn't anything Ed Searfoss can't do when it comes to glassing surfboards.

Not enough can be said about Ed Searfoss for his major contributions to surfing, especially big wave surfing and the fact that he has and continues to stoke out 10's of thousands of surfers with his glass work.

Legendary RESPECT.

NOTABLE BIG WAVE SURFERS

"Land divides, Ocean connects."
~Milton Willis

Surfers who ride big waves are often driven by a combination of factors, including personal challenge, thrill seeking, and a desire to push the limits of what is possible. Riding big waves requires a high level of skill, experience, physical fitness, and many surfers are motivated by the challenge of mastering this difficult and dangerous sport.

In addition to the personal challenge, riding big waves also provides an intense adrenaline rush. The sheer size and power of the waves can create a thrilling and exhilarating experience for surfers, and many seek out this rush as a way to escape from the stresses and pressures of everyday life.

Surfing big waves is also a way for surfers to push the limits of what is possible in the sport. By tackling bigger and more challenging waves, surfers push the boundaries of what is considered normal or even possible, and in doing so, they can inspire others to do the same. This drive to innovate and explore new frontiers is the hallmark of Hawaiian big wave surfing.

To qualify as being a legitimate big wave surfer individuals must paddle themselves into waves 20 feet or higher and make it. The following list of notable big wave surfers are legitimately qualified.

There's no such thing as PhD for big wave surfing however, if there were these guys would be PhD's many times over. Legitimate big wave surfers know their subject inside and out…. Life depends on it.

A hui hou…

Joseph "Scooter Boy" Kaopuiki HI –

Big wave surfing pioneer elder known for his high-performance surfing, creativity and pure raw hotdogging talent.

John Peck CA –

Pipeline elder known for being amongst the first to ride inside the tube as a regular footer. Expresses surfing as the action art of riding a wave of energy, leaving only a disappearing wake behind…

Eddie Aikau - native Hawaiian

Legendary Surfer of the highest order who gave his life to save others. Iconic Big Wave Surfer, first lifeguard North shore of Oʻahu.

Clyde Aikau - native Hawaiian

The younger brother of legendary big wave surfer Eddie Aikau, Iconic Big Wave Surfer, and Winner of the prestigious Eddie Aikau Big Wave Contest.

Butch Van Artsdalen CA -

Nicknamed the first "Mr. Pipeline" for being amongst the first to really surf Pipeline. Known for his fearless hard charging surfing in the biggest and most gnarly waves on the North Shore of Oʻahu.

Bethany Hamilton HI -

World renowned for her surfing skills, courage and is among the most notable surfers in the world. Bethany has appeared in movies, documentaries, magazines, books and is a powerful motivational speaker.

Buzzy Kerbox HI -

Expert big wave surfer, founder of the modern tow surfing movement, super model for Ralph Lauren.

Laird Hamilton HI –

Quintessential expert big wave surfer, early pioneer of tow in surfing, stepson of legendary surfer Billy Hamilton.

Garrett McNamara HI –

Expert big wave surfer recognized for being the first to surf big Nazare' in Portugal and held the Guinness book of world record for surfing the biggest waves.

Roger Erickson HI -

Well respected big wave surfer. Father of big wave surfing expert Emi Erickson.

Adam Salvio HI -

Waimea Bay, Pipeline, expert big wave surfer. Known for his brave solo sessions in huge waves.

Mike Doyle CA –

Early big wave surfing pioneer. First ever to build a soft surfboard.

L.J. Richards CA –

Champion early big wave surfing pioneer.

Titus Kinimaka HI –

Champion expert big wave surfer, Living Legend, voice of Hawai'i musician.

Cheyne Horan AUS -

World Champion professional surfer, big wave surfer noted for surfing "Code Black" Biggest Wednesday January 28th, 1998, major Surfboard innovator.

Mickey "Mongoose" Munoz CA –

Known as one of the earliest surfers to surf the North Shore and big Waimea Bay.

Felipe Pomar PE -

Expert pioneer big wave surfer from Peru, first ever recognized World Champion surfer, recognized for surfing two Tsunamis.

Carlos Burle BR -

Two-time giant wave world champion, pioneered tow-in surfing after studying the Willis brothers on 1/28/89.

Jojo Roper CA –

Expert big wave surfer known for surfing huge Todos Santos Mexico and son of legendary surfer Joe Roper.

Jamilah Star CA –

Expert big wave surfer recognized for paddle surfing XXL Waimea Bay, Jaws, and Mavericks.

Johnny Boy Gomes HI –

Famous for surfing huge Waimea and Pipeline with reckless abandon and power.

Reno Abellira HI –

Recognized for surfing the swell of 1974, Waimea Bay.

Jose Angel HI -

Fearless surfer described by fellow big wave pioneer Greg Noll as "the gutsiest surfer there ever was".

Greg Noll CA/HI –

An American pioneer of big wave surfing and a prominent longboard shaper. Nicknamed "Da Bull".

David Kalama HI –

Son of surfing great Ilima Kalama. Expert big wave surfer known for surfing big Jaws on Maui and helping to pioneer tow in surfing.

Ron Barron HI -

Big wave surfer, tow-in surfer, long distance paddler and all-around respected waterman. Ace Cool's tow-in surfing partner.

Noah Johnson – HI

Expert big-wave rider from the Big Island of Hawai'i, winner of the 1999 Quiksilver in Memory of Eddie Aikau contest at Waimea Bay.

Peter Mel CA -

Expert big wave surfer, Maverick's superstar, surfing media commentator, Aikau big wave surfing contest invitee.

Tony Roy HI –

Expert big wave surfer known for surfing outer reefs.

Tom Nellis HI –

Big wave surfing expert and master surfboard shaper

Barry Kanaiapuni HI –

Expert big wave power surfer, shaper, "Surfing begins at 6 feet."

Jeff Clark CA –

Recognized as being the first big wave surfer to surf Mavericks CA and introducing Mavericks to the world.

Ted Schmidt HI –

Expert big wave surfer credited with surfing "Code Black"

Randy Rarrick HI -

Expert surfer, shaper, surfing promoter, surfboard collector, world traveler, surfing spokesman.

Liam McNamara HI -

Pipeline Master expert tube rider, one of the first surfers to do airs.

Scott Channy Chandler CA -

Expert big wave surfer, stand out in Hawai'i, California and Todos Santos, Garrett McNamara's first tow in partner for Cortez Banks, expert surfboard shaper, true hero.

Joel Vigiano NY -

Expert big wave surfer from New York, credited with surfing Waimea at 25 feet on a 7'4" surfboard (50 feet by today's standards).

Takao Kuga JPN -

Five-time Japanese Professional Surfing Association champion (1982, 1984–87). Expert Big Wave Surfer, Eddie Aikau big wave surfing contest invitee.

Ritchie Schmidt CA -

Expert big wave surfer, Stand out in Hawai'i and California, Lifeguard, surf coach, Aikau big wave contest invitee.

Dennis Pang HI -

Expert big wave surfer, extraordinary surfboard shaper, and a good man.

Jorge Paccelli BR -

Expert big wave surfer, known for outstanding backside performances at extreme big third Reef Pipeline.

Andy St. Onge HI -

Big wave surfing expert North Shore O'ahu. Known for riding big surfboards in big waves.

Clark Abbey - HI

Big wave surfing expert, Hawaiian champion, and a good man.

Makua Rothman HI -

Expert big wave surfer known for surfing waves estimated 60 feet at Jaws aka Pe'ahi Maui, popular musician.

Robbie Page AUS -

Expert big wave surfer, Waimea, Sunset Beach, and Pipeline, winner Pipeline Master's surfing contest in Hawai'i, and the Star in the movies North Shore and Rolling Thunder.

Tony Moniz HI -

Expert big wave surfer, Hawaiian champion, man of God.

Mike Parsons CA –

Expert big wave surfer pioneered huge Cortez Banks, K2 Big Wave $50,000 prize winner, and former Guinness book of world records holder for the largest wave ever surfed.

Peter Davi CA –

Known as the prince of big waves, recognized for surfing huge waves at Waimea Bay, Pipeline, and California.

Jaime Sterling HI -

Expert big wave surfer, son of surfing standout Doug Sterling.

Ivan Trent HI -

Big wave surfing expert, Waimea Bay stand out, navy seal, son of legendary big wave surfer Buzzy Trent.

Betty Depolito HI -

Pioneer big wave surfing for women, founder big wave surfing contest for women Queen of the Bay.

Pat Curren CA/HI -

Legendary big wave surfing pioneer, father of World Champion Surfer Tom Curren, big wave gun pioneer and original curse breaker at Waimea Bay.

Chris Owens HI -

Expert big wave surfer, marathon paddler.

Jaime O'Brian HI -

Expert surfer, first to be recognized for ripping Pipeline on a soft surfboard, YouTube superstar.

Michael Ho, Derek Ho, Mason Ho, Coco Ho HI –

Big wave surfing experts, legendary, surfing ohana, all top pros.

Kit Horn CA -

Pioneer big wave surfer known for surfing huge San Francisco waves underneath the Golden Gate Bridge.

Brian Keaulana HI -

Son of the legendary Buffalo Keaulana, 2022 Hawai'i Waterman Hall of Fame Inductee, featured in Big Wave Guardians movie 2022, Expert big wave surfer, Hawaiian lifeguard, ocean safety expert.

Eric Hass HI -

Expert big wave surfer known for surfing the biggest days solo and taking off in the most critical positions on the biggest waves.

Derrick Doerner HI -

Expert big wave surfing expert, lifeguard who doubled for Patrick Swayze in the Point Break movie where he took the wipeouts.

Brock Little HI -

Expert big wave surfer, movie stunt double

Greg Long CA -

An American surfer won the Quiksilver Big Wave Surfing Invitational in memory of Eddie Aikau at

Waimea Bay, the Red Bull Titans of Mavericks event held at Mavericks in Northern California, and the Red Bull Big Wave Africa event held at Dungeons in Hout Bay, South Africa.

Peter Cole HI -

Pioneer big wave surfing, expert swimmer, mathematician.

Billy Kemper HI -

Jaws aka Pe'ahi Maui stand out, family man.

Gary Linden CA -

Expert big wave surfer and world-renowned master shaper.

Charlie Walker HI -

Expert big wave surfer, accomplished surfboard sander.

Shane Dorian HI -

Expert big wave surfer, movie star 'In God's Hands'.

Herbie Fletcher, Nathen Fletcher, Christian Fletcher, Walter Hoffman, Flippy Hoffman, Marty Hoffman, Joyce Hoffman CA/HI -

Surfing experts and surfing Ohana dynasty.

Greg Russ HI/TX –

Hardcore big wave surfing expert specialized gnarly big wave surfing tube rider.

Thierry Vieilledent FR -

Big wave surfing expert, surfboard shaper, European surfing legend.

James Jones HI -

Expert big wave surfing expert, gentleman and first surfer to be recorded getting barreled at Waimea Bay, expert shaper.

Ken Bradshaw HI -

Expert big wave surfer, expert surfboard shaper, famous for the iconic photo taken by Hank Fotos on Jan 28th, 1998.

Craig Elmer "Owl" Chapman, Gary Chapman, Sam Hawk, and Dick Brewer HI -

Expert big wave surfers, expert shapers, major contributors of the modern surfboard.

Kai Lenny HI -

Big wave surfing expert, extreme big wave expert, television star, surfing super star.

Luke Shepardson HI -

Big wave surfing expert, lifeguard, winner of the prestigious Eddie Aikau big wave surfing contest.

Ross Clark Jones AUS -

Big wave surfing expert, extreme big wave expert, noted for Surfing Biggest Wednesday "Code Black" January 28th, 1998.

Dan Moore HI -

Big wave surfing expert, Billabong XXL Global Big Wave Winner - Outer Reef 2006, and $50,000 prize money.

Don Curry CA -

Big wave surfing expert, pioneer of Ghost Tree big wave surfing spot of Pebble Beach, Carmel California.

Brad Gerlach CA –

Former professional rank surfer known for pioneering huge Cortez Banks off the coast of California.

Ed Guzman CA -

Big wave surfing expert, surfing coach, pioneer Ghost Tree big wave surfing spot.

Tony Ray AUS -

Big wave surfing expert, noted for surfing Biggest Wednesday "Code Black" January 28th, 1998.

Peter Townend "PT" AUS/CA –

Big wave surfing expert, known for his pink surfboards and being first professional world surfing champion, doubled for William Katt in the Hollywood movie Biggest Wednesday.

Gerry Lopez – HI

Expert big wave surfer known for surfing extreme Pipeline and being amongst the first to tow surf huge Jaws on Maui

Taylor Knox CA -

Big wave surfing expert, first Guinness book of world records for biggest wave ever surfed, winner $50,000 K2 big wave contest.

The Silver Surfer, the World -

Dedicated to all the surfers who've ever gone surfing and didn't get their photo taken and didn't have anyone see their waves, they went out there alone not seeking fortune or fame just for the thrill of it.

"If the tree falls in the forest and no one sees it, did it fall?" Laird Hamilton

RENOWNED
BIG WAVE SURFING PHOTOGRAPHERS

"The art of capturing life in motion."
~Aaron Chang

Amongst the most skilled action sports photographers in the world has to include big wave surfing photographers.

Certainly, some of the most jaw dropping exciting and spectacular images ever captured on film come from the world of big wave surfing.

Big wave surfing photographers are dedicated and highly skilled at what they do, often risking their own lives by being right out there in the danger zone in order to get front and center up close pics of the world's biggest waves and the surfers who ride them.

Photographers that take pictures of big wave surfing have to be motivated by something more than money to do what they do. Economically taking pictures of big waves is a difficult way to make a living.

Big wave photographers must be passionate about what they do. The real payoff comes in the form of historical legacy. An epic all time ride may last less than 30 seconds but a picture of that ride can go on indefinitely.

The following is a partial list of the world's best photographers who have visually captured the thrills, chills, and spills of big wave surfing throughout the years for the world to see for years to come. Big Respect.

Bud Brown -

One of the earliest photographers to document big wave surfing at Pipeline, Sunset Beach and Waimea Bay from the beginning.

Hank Fotos -

Known for risking it all to get the shot. Hank took the historic photo of Ken Bradshaw on 1/28/98.

Shirley Rogers –

Shirley Rogers a photographer on the North Shore capturing the best surfers on the best waves since the early 70's. Beautiful and exotic, Rogers also appeared in front of the camera on television, in movies, books and magazines.

Vince Cavataio -

Water photographer known for filming Hawaii's biggest and most dangerous waves up close and beautiful women when the surf is flat.

Brian Bielman -

Award winning photographer with over four decades of capturing images of big waves in Hawai'i and worldwide, His images have appeared on over 150 covers and in periodicals from Surfing to Rolling Stone magazines.

Dan Merkle -

Best known for high impact still photography, primary water photographer for Surfing magazine in the 70's.

Aaron Chang -

Award Winning photographer, 25 years Surfing magazine senior photographer specializing in surfing fine ocean art images.

Deniro Sato -

Water photographer from Japan credited with over 30 years of documenting big waves worldwide including a famous picture of Gerry Lopez where a Hawaiian face can be seen in the wave.

Alberto Sodre' -

Brazilian photographer who captured some of the best images of the North Shore big wave surfing especially Waimea Bay.

Warren Bolster -

Surfing and skateboarding photographer credited with capturing Alec Cooke, aka Ace Cool's, epic 100 FOOT WAVE.

Tim Bonithon -

Known for filming big wave documentaries including historic Biggest Wednesday, January 28th, 1998.

Art Brewer -

Photographer's photographer visually chronicling big waves worldwide beginning mid 60's, former photo editor for Surfer magazine.

Larry Haynes -

Respected big wave photographer known for recording the world's best surfers in the most dangerous waves up close from the water.

BIG WAVE SURFBOARDS & TOW-IN SURFBOARD DESIGN

"You don't go hunting Rhinos with a BB gun."
~Buzzy Trent

The main difference between a big wave gun surfboard, and a big wave tow-in surfboard is the overall volume and tow surfboards are equipped with tow straps.

Big wave gun surfboards are designed for surfers to paddle into fast moving often hollow big waves. Several performance characteristics include:

-      Extra length and width

-      Increased volume

-      Floatation and surface planning enabling design for optimum paddle ability required to reach speeds fast enough to catch big waves.

Although padding is increased maneuverability is sacrificed. Big wave guns can be difficult to turn and control. The Rocker or bottom curve is of paramount importance. Not enough entry rocker hampers a big wave guns ability to make that last second and extra steep drops. Too much nose entry (bow) rocker will push water on a big wave gun causing it to be difficult to catch big waves.

Big wave surfboards are generally flat though the center or very low curve for speed. The Tail (stern) rockers vary. The lower the curve through the tail the faster the surfboard will go, but again the sacrifice is maneuverability.

In contrast, big wave tow-in surfboards could be referred to as mini-guns, as they are scaled down to the minimum versions of the big wave gun. With the aid of a jet ski paddling is no longer the first priority. Instead, speed and maneuverability are.

Tow-in big wave surfboards are several feet smaller than the traditional big wave gun and very narrow and thin in comparison allowing for maximum speed, control, and maneuverability.

Tow-in surfboards are also equipped with foot straps to help the surfer stay attached to the board at the highest speeds and in the roughest and turbulent of conditions which allows the surfer to use their feet to help steer and control the surfboard.

The big wave surfboards the Willis brothers rode on January 25th, 1998, "Code Black I" were as follows:

Milton Willis was surfing a 10'6" x 21" x 3.5"

Glassed on three-fin set up (Tom A. Hawk designer fins)

Medium entry rocker with extra curve at the tip.

Weight approximately 15 lbs.

Michael Willis was surfing a 10' 0" x 20.75" x 3.25"

Glassed on three-fin set up (Tom A. Hawk designer fins)

Medium rocker.

Weight approximately 14 lbs.

Airbrushed by Australian Paul Fullbrook.

Big wave tow-in surfboards that the Willis brothers surfed on January 28th, 1998, "Code Black II":

First session Outer Log Cabins:

Milton was surfing a 7'2" x 17" x 2.25"

Equipped with foot straps.

Glassed on three-fin set up (Tom A. Hawk designer fins)

Approximately 12 lbs.

Airbrushed by Australian Paul Fullbrook.

Second session Outer Log Cabins and DEVIL's GARDEN:

Milton and Michael surfed a 7'2" x 17.25" x 2.25"

Equipped with foot straps.

Glassed on three-fin set up (Tom A. Hawk designer fins)

Chambered and BBs added.

Approximate weight 15 lbs.

Chapter 18

HAWAIIAN WORDS & THEIR DEFINITIONS

"Ua Mau ke Ea o ka ʻĀina i ka Pono
the life of the land is perpetuated
in righteousness."
~Hawaiʻi State Motto

A hui hou...
Until we meet again

Aina...
Land

Akumai...
Intelligent, smart

Alii...
Royalty

Aloha...
Love, hello and goodbye
literally the presence of breath

Aloha ke Akua...
God is Love

Amakua...
Familial guardians or ancestors who can assume the
form of animals, plants or other forms occurring in
nature.

E kipa mai...
To invite someone to visit.

E komo mai...
Invitation to enter your house.

Haole...

Breathless or a person of non-Hawaiian heritage generally associated with a white person.

Hale...
House

Hanai...
Adopted Family

Hauoli...
Happy

Hoihi...
Respect

Hoku...
Star

Hooponopono...
A traditional Hawaiian practice of reconciliation and forgiveness.

Hui...
A club or association

Hukilau...
A way of fishing invented by early Hawaiians.

Ikaika...
Warrior

Imua...
An urging forward

Kahuna...
A wise man/shaman, literally "the Secret"

Kai...
Ocean

Kala...
Money

Kalohe...
Rascal

Kamaaina...
Native

Kanaka Maoli...
Indigenous person

Kane...
Man

Kapu...
Forbidden, off limits.

Kapuna...
Elder

Lanikai...

Heavenly sea

Laniakea...
Immeasurable Heaven

Lei...
A flower necklace symbolizing love and friendship

Mahalo...
Thank you!

Makai...
Ocean side

Malahini...
Newcomer

Malama...
Take care!

Mana...
Spiritual power

Manini...
Small or little

Mano...
Shark

Mauka...
Mountain side

Mele...
Chants, songs or poems, happy

Menehune...
Mythological race of dwarf people

Moi moi...
Sleep

Nalu...
Wave

No ka oi...
The best

Oʻahu...
The gathering place

Ohana...
Family

Ono...
Delicious

Paumalu...
Taken by surprise

Pau...
Finished

Pau hanna...
Work finished

Pilau...
Stinky

Pono...
Righteous

Puka...
Hole

Pule...
Prayer, blessing

Wahine...
Woman

Welina...
A greeting of affection, similar to aloha

Wikiwiki...
Hurry

Photographic Gallery and Evidence

Duke Paoa Kahanamoku

Team Surfboard Hawai'i Little League

Milton front row, Michael second row, John Price team sponsor, surfer and Surfboards Hawaii owner/shaper back row.

Solana Beach, CA

Michael Willis

Sunset Surfboards

Encintas, CA

Michael Willis

Sunset Surfboards, Encintas, CA

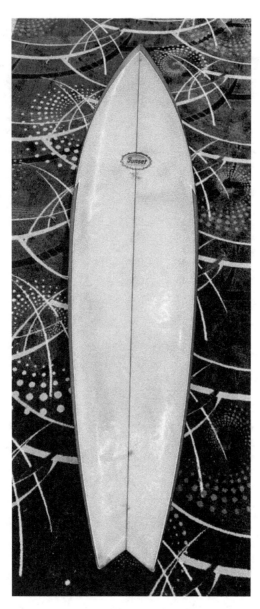

Michael Willis

Sunset Surfboards, Encintas, CA

Willis Brothers Surf Shop

Hale‘iwa, Hawai‘i

Michael Willis shaping bay

Sunset Point, Hawaiʻi

Photo: Brian Bielmann

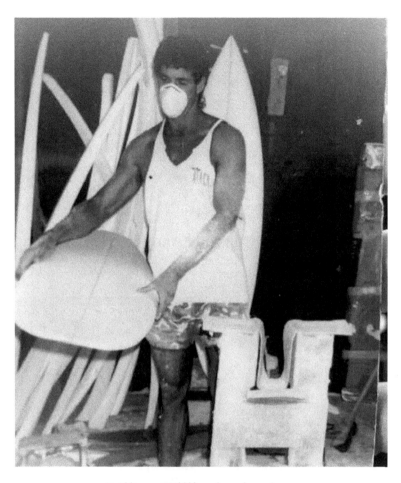

Milton Willis shaping bay

Sunset Beach, Hawai'i

Brothers in Arms ---

Bruce Irons and Andy Irons

Michael Willis and Milton Willis

Photo: Brooks Sullivan

"Banzai Betty" Depolito

Sunset Beach, Hawai'i

Photo: Shirley Rogers

Willis brothers,

Waimea Bay

Photo: Paul Gordinho

Ace Cool's leap of faith

Photo: Warren Bolster

The Biggest Wave

Ace Cool - first 100 FOOT WAVE ever surfed and documented.

Photo: Warren Bolster

Johnny Boy Gomes, Milton Willis, Peter Davi

Waimea Bay from the book Surfers

Milton Willis paddle in

Waimea Bay

Photo: Brian Bielmann

Milton Willis

Code Black I

Jason Magers

Code Black II

Jason Magers, Code Black II

Photo: John Bilderback

Michael and Milton, Code Black II

Outer Log Cabins

Ken Bradshaw, Code Black II, Outer Log Cabins

Photo: Hank Fotos

Michael Willis sketch

Artist: Terry Lamb

Michael Willis

Backyards, Sunset Point Hawai'i

Cheyne Horan, Robbie Page

Waimea Bay, North Shore Oʻahu

Duane le Compte

Duane le Compte

Willis Brothers Big Wave Guns

North Shore

Milton and Michael Willis, Hale'iwa

Photo: Andy Martin, from the book Walking on Water

Michael Willis

Paddle in, Ghost Tree, Pebble Beach, CA

Willis Brothers collage, North Shore Hawai'i

Michael Willis, Marty Hoffman, Milton Willis

Big Wave Guardians premiere, Oceanside, CA

Email from the United States Lifesaving Association (USLA) thanking the Willis brothers and confirming the Hawaiian Surfers Way to survive rip currents has been incorporated in pictograph format.

From: USLA <webmaster@usla.org>

Date: Mon, Feb 24, 2020, 6:03 AM

Thank you for your input and interest in saving lives at surf beaches. The USLA and our partners at NOAA occasionally review and revise our rip current safety messaging in accordance with the latest science and input from experts worldwide. After a meticulous, two-year review, we have revised the signs, brochures, and posters accordingly. As part of the review process, input was gathered from social scientist, educators, oceanographers, lifeguards, and many others among our partners at NOAA. You had previously provided input to encourage people caught in a rip current to swim toward breaking waves. This was consistent with some other messaging we reviewed and considered prudent, so the new advice includes that in a pictograph format.

Signs and other educational materials we provide are printed and posted by local governments. They tend to be left posted until they are worn out - a process that can take many years. Therefore, we avoid making changes unless the reasons are soundly based in science. After the time consuming update process we would imagine that future changes will not be made for several years. (The interval between the last two updates was about 12 years.) Thank you for your input, particularly your prior input, which was incorporated.

Thank you, United States Lifesaving Association

Think Waves: Milton Willis and Michael Willis Clear Up Rip Current Confusion

SAN DIEGO, May 13, 2021 /PRNewswire/ -- Each year hundreds of people drown in the ocean and tens of thousands are rescued by Lifeguards and Surfers.

Whether you are a surfer, swimmer or casual beach goer this is valuable information.

Surfers, Milton and Michael, the Willis brothers are on a mission to drastically reduce ocean drownings and rescues. Their plan is to share with the world the Surfers Way to escape rip currents by using waves.

Today it is generally accepted there are three viable options for surviving rip currents. Swim parallel to the beach (advocated by lifeguards), let the rip take you (endorsed by oceanographer Dr. Jaime MacMahan), and go towards the waves (promoted by long time surfers Milton and Michael Willis).

Though NOAA and USLA have done a great job picto-graphically posting signs showing rip current escape options, most beach goers remain unaware waves will take them back to shore.

For hundreds of years experienced surfers have used rip currents to get beyond the breakers to surf, riding waves to get back to shore.

Watch experienced surfers such as Gerry Lopez, Kelly Slater and Allen Sarlo surfing, they paddle out with the rip and ride waves back to shore. Perfect examples of the Surfers Way.

"When it comes to escaping rip currents, whether you swim parallel or let it take you out, there is no other way to get back to shore other than using waves and the general public needs to be educated," explains Milton Willis.

Tried, true, proven simple and effective, the Surfers Way of escaping rip currents using waves has been called "the world's greatest intuitive self-rescue technique" by Seabright N. J. Lifeguard Captain Michael Hutchinson.

The Willis Bros are advocating City and State Officials nation wide post the words Rips Out, Waves In on signs along with the pictograph formatting. Educating the public is key.

"Informing beach goers to avoid rip currents by wading or swimming in front of waves and to escape rip currents by swimming towards the nearest waves will dramatically reduce rescues and save lives." says Michael Willis

The Willis brothers have taught others the Surfers Way to escape rip currents through videos, posters, PSA's and in educational settings such as surfing lessons and ocean safety clinics.

For more information about the Surfers Way to Escape Rip Currents visit ThinkWaves.org

#ThinkWaves #NOAA #RipCurrents

Willis Brothers Think Waves

PR Newswire

Michael Willis sharing the Hawaiian Surfers Way for surviving rip currents.

Ocean Beach Lifeguard Headquarters, CA

Titus Kinimaka rescue Waimea Bay

"The most dramatic rescue in surfing history"

Surfing 100 Foot Waves

Willis Brothers Interview

As time goes on, the Willis brothers Milton and Michael become more and more mythical for their world-famous surfing adventures, trials and tribulations, including surfing 100 foot plus waves. One big step forward for extreme big wave surfing, one giant leap forward for humanity. The following three questions get into the heart and soul of the only two humans alive to actually been proven to surf 100 foot waves.

What's it like? Find out in their own words…

Question: Milton, what did you get out of this experience?

> **Milton:** *First and foremost, was the immediate physical gratification the excitement the adrenaline the rush the thrill. Wow!!!*

> *It's like your happy place, you're feeling really alive that's what I first got out of it.*

Question: How did this make you feel?

> **Milton:** *Small and insignificant being exposed to that great of power, greater than all the intensity of eternity in that heartbeat of a*

215

moment. I felt a deep connection to a Higher Power.

Question: What message do you have for others?

Milton: *My message is that whatever you're doing it will be greater if you tie yourself to a cause. When you do something that deserves attention, positive or negative, many people do negative things to call attention to a cause; anytime you do something that deserves attention, eyeballs, it's your responsibility to attach it to a cause. My cause is saving lives through ocean safety education specifically how to survive rip currents the surfer's way ... rips out waves in.*

My purpose is not to say look at me I'm the best, my purpose is to say look at you be the best you can be. If Milton can do this imagine what you can do.

Question: Michael, what did you get out of this experience?

Michael: *A deeper understanding and appreciation of the human condition body, mind and soul. My entire life's journey had prepared me and brought me to this monumental and historic moment. I could not have planned it so perfectly, nor ever dreamed I, Michael Willis, would one day surf a 100 foot wave.*

I had the realization that everything is set in motion by God's hand, the burning sun, wind, waves, and our lives. I am aware that everything we go through is preparing us for future challenges and untold future events. And finally, the importance of not only living in the now but connecting truly connecting with your Higher Power in the now.

Question: How did this make you feel?

Michael: *Humble. To accomplish riding a 100 foot wave is nothing short of a miracle. It was never my goal to surf a 100 foot wave, I was chosen to do it. I believe we are all chosen for the greater good, to live for Divine purposes beyond our comprehension.*

Surfing a 100 foot wave I felt a sense of human connection and advancement as if mankind could see through my eyes. A breakthrough for not only extreme big wave surfing but also for mankind. Time has proven me right. Surfers today chase the dream of surfing a 100 foot wave because now it's accepted as possible. We showed them the way.

Question: What message do you have for others?

Michael: *Trust in your personal Higher Power and let love guide you. Love will give you the strength and courage to overcome seemingly* *insurmountable obstacles and difficult challenges. With love everything is possible I'm proof and so are you.*

Acknowledgements

100 FOOT WAVE, Kingdom of Hawai'i, the official book would not have been possible without the following people who've contributed immensely to making this happen.

Beginning with our parents, Milton Eugene Willis and Sandra Willis, for whom without them we would've never been here in the first place.

Patty Willis and Billena Willis for being there during this historic trail blazing time in big wave surfing history. They loved it as much as we did.

Ed Searfoss for service and quality above and beyond. Ed glassed the surfboards that the Willis Brothers used on "Code Black I", January 25th, 1998, and on "Code Black II", January 28th, 1998.

Robbie Page for locating and pointing out Outer Log Cabins in the first place which turned out to be a great warm up for the bigger waves further out at Outside Paumalu. And the world should know, Robbie Page named the Holy Grail of Extreme Big Wave Surfing the World's Biggest Waves, DEVIL's GARDEN.

Kurt Moran, aka Katalyst, for his sincere friendship and for his major contribution, proofreading, and editing. It was Kurt's idea to write this book.

We also want to thank and acknowledge Mother Ocean and the Kingdom of Hawai'i, home of Extreme Big Wave Surfing, the first 100 FOOT WAVE ever photographed, and the biggest waves ever surfed to date.

And finally, THANKS and PRAISE to the Highest Power that flows through us. The same Highest Power behind the 100 FOOT WAVE. Everything with Love

Aloha ke Akua

Milton Bradley Willis and Michael Clebert Willis

About The Authors

Milton Bradley Willis –

World Champion Extreme Big Wave Surfer, philosopher, author, musician, and Ocean Safety Expert. Goals, to have a positive impact on the community and leave the world a better place.

Michael Clebert Willis -

World Champion Extreme Big Wave Surfer, author, musician, philosopher, Ocean Safety Expert, and father of three beautiful girls.

Other Books by The Authors

Discover the Greatness in You:

Words of Wisdom and Empowerment to Help You Become the Person You Are Meant to Be. by Milton B. Willis and Michael C. Willis,

Publisher: Blue Mountain Press

TIDAL WAVES: Wet and Wild Surfing Stories

Through a series of gripping stories, readers will be transported to different corners of the world, from the surfer's paradise of Hawai'i to remote shores of imagination, and they'll be introduced to an inspiring cast of surfers, each with their own unique story of tribulations and triumphs.

STRONG CURRENTS: Wet and Wild Surfing Stories

STRONG CURRENTS is a book about the spirit of surfing, Aloha, and positivity. As you sit down to read STRONG CURRENTS, you may not be quite sure what to expect. Yes, what follows is a collection of surfing tales, but what you will find within these pages is so much more than that. STRONG CURRENTS is about Wet and Wild Surfing Stories based on true life experiences.

All are available on Amazon Books and better bookstores everywhere.

Recommended further reading

100 FOOT WAVE

This book is written with the spirit of Aloha.

The purpose of this book is to save lives.

Recommended for further reading...

The Secret Science of Miracles by Max Freedom Long

Autobiography of a Yogi by Paramahansa Yogananda

The Bible, The Iliad, and the Odyssey

Love and Respect All,

Milton Bradley Willis

Michael Clebert Willis

Contact the Willis Brothers at 100ftPlusSurf.com and at Thinkwaves.org/home a 501(c)3 non-profit website to learn more about ocean safety consulting, obtain a free download of the Think Waves Poster, and make a donation.